6f

GW00726824

EN DIRECT!

Communicative Skills
for GCSE and S Grade French

Jean-Claude Gilles

John Murray

Pupils' Book   ISBN 0 7195 4370 3
Teachers' Resource Book   ISBN 0 7195 4371 1
Cassettes ISBN 0 7195 4372 X

Author's note

This is the **Pupils' Book** for **En Direct!**, providing individual, paired and group activities to help students preparing for GCSE or other communicative examinations. It is designed to be used in conjunction with the cassette tapes, which contain the spoken material for the listening sections of each unit, and with the **Teachers' Resource Book**, which contains a great deal of additional material, much of it designed to be photocopied, including extra tasks (many of them games and puzzles), a continuous assessment chart, scripts of the listening material, selected answers, and a complete Assessment Test with a GCSE mark scheme. There is also a sheet of examination advice for candidates — in English, but with a French title, *'Ecoute nos conseils'*.

A full introduction for teachers appears in the **Teachers' Resource Book**.

I should like to acknowledge the advice and help given to me in preparing **En Direct!** by Dr Yvonne Burne, Murray's modern languages adviser. A list of detailed acknowledgements appears on p128 of this book.

J-C.G.

© Jean-Claude Gilles 1987
First published 1987
Reprinted 1988 (twice), 1990
by John Murray (Publishers) Ltd
50 Albemarle Street, London W1X 4BD

All rights reserved.
Unauthorised duplication
contravenes applicable laws.

Designed and typeset by
Gecko Limited, Bicester, Oxon

Printed in Great Britain by
The Bath Press, Avon

British Library Cataloguing in Publication Data

Gilles, Jean-Claude
 En Direct: communicative skills for
 GCSE French.
 Pupils' book
 1. French language — Textbooks for
 foreign speakers — English
 I. Title
 448 PC2112
 ISBN 0-7195-4370-3

CONTENTS

1 BASIC Listening

PERSONAL BACKGROUND, DAILY ROUTINE AND SCHOOL

1 Your future exchange partner has sent you a tape, introducing himself and his family. The tape is in sections. You will hear each section twice. Then answer the question.

Section 1

What is your partner's nickname?

Section 2

When is his birthday?

Section 3

How many sisters does he have?

Section 4

Who is the youngest in the family?

Section 5

What does his father do for a living?

Section 6

At school, in which class is your partner?

Section 7

How far from school does your partner live?

Section 8

How large is your partner's house?

2 Your class and a class in the Lycée et Collège de l'Arc have been sending each other tapes for some time. On each tape, members of the class speak about a different topic. You have just received another tape. This time the topic is school work. Each pupil says what he or she thinks of different subjects.

The tape you will hear is an extract of the tape your class has just received from the Lycée et Collège de l'Arc. It is recorded in sections. You will hear each section twice. Copy the grid below, and as you listen to the tape, enter the subjects described by each person according to what that person says about them.

	I love	I like	It's OK	I don't like	I hate
Section 1 Martine					
Section 2 Jacques					
Section 3 Thierry					
Section 4 Chantal					

3 On this tape, five people talk about their jobs. Listen to the tape to work out which job from the list below each person does. You will hear each job description twice. When you have decided, write a, b, or c according to your choice.

Section 1

a) bricklayer
b) house-to-house rep
c) estate agent

Section 2

a) secretary
b) machinist
c) writer

Section 3

a) teacher
b) cleaner
c) caretaker

Section 4

a) mechanic
b) petrol pump attendant
c) garage owner

Section 5

a) surgeon
b) doctor
c) nurse

Imagine this is your first visit to a French school. You have gone to lessons with your exchange partner. Before the first lesson, the teacher reads the daily *bulletin* to the class. It includes notices to pupils, requests by teachers to see particular pupils, lost or found school equipment, etc. Read the questions before the tape starts, and write down the answers to each question after the second playing.

1 a) Who does the music teacher wish to see?
   b) Why does he wish to see them?
2 a) Do the English pupils have to pay for their meals?
   b) What do they have to do if they do not want a school meal?
3 a) What is the content of the school bag that was lost yesterday?
   b) For what reasons are pupils asked to contact the deputy headmaster?
4 a) What message does M. Durand want to give his pupils?
   b) What will pupils normally taught by him have to do tomorrow?
5 a) Who does M. Chambert want to see?
   b) What is the purpose of the meeting?

M. Boullet and Mr Collins, the French and English teachers leading an exchange, are being interviewed by the French local radio station. Listen carefully to the interview, which has been divided into three sections. You will hear each section twice. Read the questions before the tape starts, and write down the answers to each section after the second playing.

Section 1

1 Explain how the exchange has developed this year.
2 How many children are involved in the exchange?
3 How long does the exchange last?

Section 2

4 What is the composition of the British party?
5 Outline the activities involved in the exchange.
6 Will the French pupils visit their British counterparts during term-time?

Section 3

7 What expense do the participants' families have to meet?
8 Name two advantages of this exchange.
9 How does the interviewer conclude the interview? Mention four things.

BASIC Speaking 1

1 Work in pairs. Ask each other these questions in French:

1. Comment tu t'appelles?
2. Quel âge as-tu?
3. Où habites-tu?
4. Est-ce que tu as des frères et des sœurs?
5. Comment s'appellent-ils/elles?
6. Quel âge a-t-il/a-t-elle/ont-ils/ont-elles?
7. Qu'est-ce qu'ils/elles font dans la vie?
8. Quelle est la date de ton anniversaire?
9. Comment fêtes-tu ton anniversaire?
10. Où est-ce que tu es né/e?

2 Work with a partner. One of you is phoning his/her French penfriend to tell him/her that you have just moved to 15 Highbury Grove, Sheffield, and that you have a new phone number.

FRENCH PENFRIEND
Answer the phone and ask who is phoning.

Greet your friend but ask him/her to wait while you turn off the TV.

Say you are fine. Ask why your friend is phoning.

Ask if the address has changed too.

ENGLISH-SPEAKING PUPIL
Introduce yourself.

Say hello. Ask how your friend is.

Say that you want to give your new phone number: 0742 73561.

Say yes and give your new address.

It is your first day with your exchange partner's family. Ask his/her parents :

1. If they will show you round the house.
2. The time of breakfast, lunch and evening meal.
3. If they can look after your passport.
4. Where the post office is.
5. Permission to go out in the evenings.

3 Work in pairs. A French pupil is showing his or her English penfriend a photo of the family in France. Use the list of questions and the photograph below to make conversation. One of you plays the English and the other the French penfriend.

1. Cette photo est récente?
2. Est-ce que tu as pris la photo toi-même?
3. Qui est debout?
4. Quel âge a-t-il?
5. Quel âge a ta sœur?
6. Est-ce que c'est la maison où tu habites d'habitude?
7. Et maintenant, où habites-tu, en ville ou à la campagne?
8. Qu'est-ce que tu préfères? Pourquoi?

Yesterday, you were waiting at the bus stop opposite the post office, when you saw a man running away from the post office with a bag over his shoulder. Your suspicions were confirmed when you heard shouts for help from the post office. You had time to take a good look at the offender, so you could provide the police with a good description. By following your instructions, the artist from the police department produced the drawing below. What did you tell him?

Work in pairs, playing the parts of an English-speaking pupil and his/her French exchange partner.

ENGLISH-SPEAKING PUPIL	EXCHANGE PARTNER
Introduce yourself (say hello, name, and age)	Tu as des frères et des sœurs?
Answer the question, giving details if appropriate (their names, ages, etc . . .)	Où habites-tu?
Give the name of your town/village.	Parle-moi un peu de ta ville.
Say something about your town (size, industrial, old/modern)	Qu'est-ce qu'on peut y faire?
Name two activities and give brief details.	

1 BASIC Reading

1 Read the five announcements below and answer the following questions.

1 What has recently happened to Odile and Pierre-Antoine?

2 What are M. and Mme Travouillon announcing?

3 How are M. and Mme Pierre de Gaste related to Charles?

4 Mlle Anouk du Maroussem and M. François de Bordas are getting married. Where will the ceremony take place? Give the date and time of the ceremony.

5 What is the purpose of the announcement which begins with 'Le Docteur Georges Jean Cohen'?

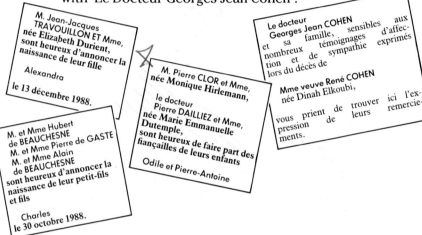

M. Pierre du Maroussem et Mme, née Claude Méry de Montigny, sont heureux de faire part du mariage de leur fille

Mlle Anouk du MAROUSSEM avec M. François de BORDAS

fils du général (c.r.) de Bordas et de Mme, née Françoise Sabatier d'Espeyran.

La cérémonie religieuse sera célébrée à Paris le vendredi 16 mars 1988, à 16 h 30, en l'église Saint-Louis des Invalides.

M. Jean-Jacques TRAVOUILLON ET Mme, née Elizabeth Durient, sont heureux d'annoncer la naissance de leur fille

Alexandra

le 13 décembre 1988.

Le docteur Georges Jean COHEN et sa famille, sensibles aux nombreux témoignages d'affection et de sympathie exprimés lors du décès de

Mme veuve René COHEN née Dinah Elkoubi,

vous prient de trouver ici l'expression de leurs remerciements.

M. Pierre CLOR et Mme, née Monique Hirlemann,

le docteur Pierre DAILLIEZ et Mme, née Marie Emmanuelle Dutemple, sont heureux de faire part des fiançailles de leurs enfants

Odile et Pierre-Antoine

M. et Mme Hubert de BEAUCHESNE M. et Mme Pierre de GASTE M. et Mme Alain de BEAUCHESNE sont heureux d'annoncer la naissance de leur petit-fils et fils

Charles le 30 octobre 1988.

2 Study the cards below and answer the questions.

What sort of licence is this?

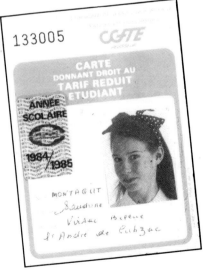

Only students can own this card. What benefit does it give them?

All adults (over 18) in France own such a card. What is its purpose?

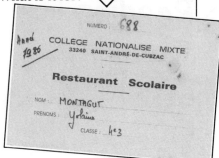

This card was given to Yolaine Montagut by her school. What is it for? ▽

What is the name of the school to which Andrée Torre belongs?

How and when can Andrée's parents be contacted in case of emergency? ▽

What is Sandrine's date of birth?
Sandrine is a student in foreign languages.
What two languages does she study?

What useful information does this card contain?

What is the purpose of this card?

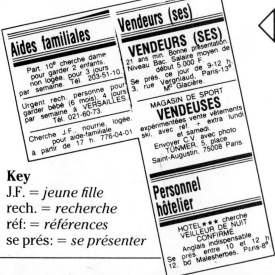

Key
J.F. = *jeune fille*
rech. = *recherche*
réf: = *références*
se prés: = *se présenter*

◁ **3** You are looking for summer employment in France. Read the advertisements.

1   As you are 16 years old, there are two jobs for which there would not be any point in applying. Which ones?

2   As you obviously are a fluent English speaker, there is a golden opportunity for you! When and where should you apply?

3   If you phoned 776-04-01, what job would you be applying for? As you would not receive any money for your services, how would you be rewarded?

4   What experience is required to work at Tunmer?

1

Read this horoscope carefully, then answer the questions.

1 Give the French for
   a) Gemini
   b) Aries
   c) Aquarius
   d) Libra
2 Write in English what is predicted for your own sign.
3 If you were born at the end of March, the 30th is your lucky day. What do they say is likely to happen to you?
4 Explain the problems Scorpios are likely to encounter this week.
5 In what way can Leos expect this week to be favourable?
6 Will anything special happen to Cancerians this week?
7 Capricornians will enjoy a good week. What can they expect?
8 Will the 28th be a good day for Pisces?
9 What kind of problems can Sagittarians expect on the 3rd?
10 Virgoans' social life is very promising this week. Explain.
11 Life is full of contradictions for Taureans. On what level?

BELIER
21 mars-19 avril

☐ Quelques problèmes cette semaine en particulier les 28 et 29 qui risquent de vous apporter des déceptions, des complications en affaires ou sur le plan légal ou fiscal, des manœuvres dont vous pourriez être victime. Heureusement, sur le plan affectif, il y aura d'excellents moments, surtout le 30, favorisant des amitiés amoureuses, des flirts, des succès...

TAUREAU
20 avril-20 mai

☐ Beaucoup de contradictions dans votre existence cette semaine et plus particulièrement le 3 où, sur le plan affectif, vous risquez à la fois de « partir » comme une fusée, pleine d'espoir et d'illusions, d' «y croire » dur comme fer et de vous apercevoir en même temps, une fois de plus, que dès qu'on est amoureux, on est en état de stress! Chance, par ailleurs, certaine.

GEMEAUX
21 mai-20 juin

☐ Le 3 vous place encore une fois en face de choix impossibles, déconcertants. Il vous faudra improviser réagir très vite, à un moment où cela vous sera particulièrement difficile parce que vous aurez la tête pleine de doutes et d'incertitudes. Le 4 vous trouverez auprès d'un ami un conseil utile, surtout s'il est Bélier. Ou bien il vous entraînera efficacement.

CANCER
21 juin-21 juillet

☐ Il ne se passera rien d'exceptionnel dans votre existence cette semaine si ce n'est que reviennent des souvenirs du passé, avec la nostalgie qui les accompagne. Vos désirs seront très contradictoires. Une part de vous-même aura envie d'accueillir ces êtres qui remontent de votre mémoire et une autre s'en méfiera, par peur de réveiller de vieilles souffrances ou blessures.

LION
22 juillet-22 août

☐ Plutôt bonne, cette semaine qui devrait vous assurer un brillant succès dans une démarche ou dans une entreprise. La chance est avec vous le 3 surtout, surtout si vous voulez vous assurer des appuis puissants, des protections. Investissements positifs ou réussite dans une affaire litigieuse. Mais le 4 fait craindre soit une grosse fatigue, en contre-coup, soit un frein brutal.

VIERGE
23 août-22 septembre

☐ Vous jouirez d'une vie sociale agréable, avec plus de rencontres ou de sorties, davantage de contacts agréables, peut-être même une amitié amoureuse qui vous causera de la joie, le 30. Vous trouverez du plaisir dans la présence d'un Bélier stimulant. Le 4 est également favorable. Un Gémeaux vous amusera et vous travaillerez sans doute très bien pour vous-même, intellectuellement.

BALANCE
23 septembre-22 octobre

☐ Vous essaierez de vous distraire un peu, de sortir, de rencontrer des amis et d'entreprendre avec eux des choses sympathiques à partager : balades, vacances, escapades, activités sportives ou artistiques, réunions au cours desquelles on brasse beaucoup d'idées... et peu importe s'il n'en sort pas beaucoup de réalisations concrètes. L'essentiel, c'est de rêver et partager.

SCORPION
23 octobre-21 novembre

☐ La semaine est très difficile, exceptionnellement difficile. Soyez donc très prudent parce que vous vous trouverez confronté dans divers domaines à des choix douloureux, à des tensions, à des angoisses dès le 30, à de la fatigue ou à des contre-temps dès le 1er, à des complications dans la vie sentimentale. Même le 4 freine vos ambitions.

SAGITTAIRE
22 novembre-22 décembre

☐ Le 29 la chance vous sourira, en vous aidant à prendre des risques, à aller de l'avant, à tenter quelque chose de difficile qui vous aiderait follement. Et dans l'ensemble, vous serez plutôt décidé et enthousiaste. Toutefois, il y aura le 3 un sujet de contrariété, peut-être une querelle avec des amis proches ou avec un frère. Peut-être aussi, lettre préoccupante.

CAPRICORNE
23 décembre-19 janvier

☐ Il y a des soucis, certes, mais deux aspects marquent avec force votre semaine: le trigone de Jupiter au Soleil le 3 qui promet succès, victoires, encouragements et triomphes. Le 3 aussi, le trigone de Neptune à Vénus qui vous aidera à rêver, côté cœur, de mirages auxquels vous n'osiez plus croire. Vous craignez toujours de souffrir mais il faut faire confiance, parfois!

VERSEAU
20 janvier-19 février

☐ Pas grand chose à dire de cette semaine. Le 29 est positif et favorise des bonnes surprises. Il y a des hasards heureux et des chances à saisir, des gens qu'il faut prendre au mot s'ils vous font une proposition séduisante. En revanche, le 3 fait craindre quelques malentendus, quelques dissonances dans vos relations amicales. Vous ne savez pas toujours vous faire comprendre.

POISSONS
20 février-20 mars

☐ Il semble que le climat sentimental soit bon, que votre nature romanesque soit comblée. Vous rêverez, certes, mais sans trop vous faire d'illusions, en sachant simplement que vous vous autoriserez un peu à rêver, parce que vous en avez besoin. Les 30 et 3 vous seront favorables et vous feront oublier le 28 au cours duquel vous risquez fort de vous « faire avoir »!

Magazine 60 is the name of one of the latest pop groups. A journalist from *Cool* has given them an interview. Read the script of the interview and answer the questions below.

Ou Véronique, Pierre et Dominique ont ils bien pu rencontrer "Don Quichotte", on ne le sait pas mais quelle idée originale d'en faire une chanson. Né sous le signe de la bonne humeur, Magazine 60 est de ces groupes qu'il fait bon écouter, regarder, et avec qui on aime rêver de la "Costa del Sol"...

Cool: Magazine 60, c'est trois' personnes, alors présentez vous?

DOMINIQUE: J'ai 27 ans, ma passion après le métier que je fais, c'est le football. Je suis un grand sportif surtout.

VÉRONIQUE: J'ai 26 ans. En dehors de la musique et du groupe, je suis assez passionée par la mode, j'aime bien tout ce qui est fringue, maquillage, coiffure... sinon, je suis très curieuse.

PIERRE: J'ai 24 ans. Ma passion à part la musique c'est l'aventure, les voyages. J'aimerais bien faire le tour du monde mais pour le moment je n'en ai pas encore eu l'occasion. Avec les tournées on bouge pas mal, donc c'est sur la bonne voie. J'espère quand même faire un jour le tour du monde en bâteau.

Cool: Comment vous êtes-vous rencontrés et comment vous est venue l'idée de fonder le groupe Magazine 60?

MAGAZINE 60: Magazine 60, c'est venu un peu bizarrement. Pierre et moi Dominique, nous nous connaissions déjà en tant que choristes et musiciens de studio. C'est alors que nous avons eu la chance de rencontrer le producteur du groupe qui avait eu l'idée de mettre sous forme de medley tous les succès des années 60. Il nous a soumis l'idée mais il manquait d'autres chanteurs et chanteuses. Lors d'un cocktail, j'ai rencontré Véronique et je lui ai alors raconté ce que nous voulions faire. A l'époque elle était mannequin mais elle est quand même venue faire un essai en studio qui a été très vite concluant. En dehors de nous trois, il y avait aussi d'autres gens dans le groupe, mais depuis on est resté, tous les trois ensemble et ça continue.

Cool: On ne se contente pas de vous écouter chanter, il faut aussi vous regarder. Pourquoi attachez vous tant d'importance au visuel?

M. 60: Pour nous si tu veux, le fait de faire du studio, d'enregistrer des chansons, c'est très bien mais d'un autre côté il manque la petite chose de vraiment extraordinaire alors on estime que lorsqu'on fait des galas, le public vient se déranger, alors on est là pour lui en donner un peu pour son argent. Il faut faire du spectacle donc il est important d'avoir un look, une chorégraphie et quelque chose de réel à montrer sur scène.

Cool: Quel est pour vous le moment que vous préférez dans ce métier?

M. 60: C'est vrai que pour nous artistes on a toujours dit que les bravos étaient notre nourriture. Quand on est sur scène on est tout à fait une autre personne. On ne peut pas expliquer ce qu'on ressent, et quand ça marche, quand le public applaudit et chante avec nous, on a une certaine jouissance vraiment inexplicable. Je pense que c'est le moment qui nous fait vraiment vibrer.

Cool: Pourquoi avez vous choisi de chanter en Espagnol?

M. 60: Don Quichotte c'est un peu une chanson humoristique au deuxième degré alors on a estimé que c'était sympa de chanter dans la langue du personnage.

Cool: Allez vous conserver le côté clin d'oeil et justement humoristique de cette chanson?

M. 60: Oui, déjà ce qu'on garde, c'est ce côté soleil autrement dit l'Espagne. D'ailleurs l'album s'intitule "Costa Del Sol" et rien que ce nom sonne comme soleil, vacances... C'est ce que représente un peu Magazine 60. Nous ne sommes pas des artistes à messages. On fait une musique dite de danse, d'amusements. Lorsqu'on chante nos chansons, on s'amuse et apparemment le public aussi.

Cool: Vos projets?

M. 60: C'est l'actualité avec la sortie de cet album. Notre rêve à présent, faire une tournée avec des musiciens.

1   In the group, are there
    a) three boys?
    b) two boys and one girl?
    c) one boy and two girls?

2   Which of the three wants to take a trip round the world?

3   Which of the three likes fashion?

4   The group's name is Magazine 60. What is the particular significance of the number 60?

5   In which paragraph does the group explain why the way they look on stage is so important?

6   What professional reward does the group appreciate most?

7   In what language do they sing?

8   What kind of entertainment do they provide?

1 BASIC Writing

1 Write a letter of about 80 words in French to your new penfriend making the following points:

- Introduce yourself (name, age, where you live).
- Describe yourself physically (height, weight, colour of eyes, hair).
- Describe your family.
- Describe your house.
- Say what you particularly like and dislike.

2 Your penfriend has asked you for a copy of your timetable at school. Copy and complete it in French.

L'heure	Lundi	Mardi	Mercredi	Jeudi	Vendredi
Matin					
			Récréation		
			L'heure du Déjeuner		
Après - Midi					

3 As your exchange partner was out last night, his/her mother asked you to tell him/her what has to be done today. So as not to forget anything you decided that you would make written notes of her instructions. Here is roughly what she said:

Bread has to be bought

Washing up has to be done

Beds have to be made

Table has to be laid

After lunch, table has to be cleared

Sweep up the floor

Mercredi 18 juin

Matin

Après-midi

Your parents have had an excellent idea for the family holidays. If they could find a French family who would like to swap houses with them in August, the cost of holidaying abroad would be greatly reduced. They have thought of the possibility of advertising in a French newspaper and have therefore asked you to write the advertisement in French. Here are the details of your house:

- It is in the south west of England, 100 miles from London

- It is outside town – on bus route to town (bus stop in front of your house)

- 3 bedrooms – 1 kitchen – 1 dining room – 1 lounge – 1 bathroom – 1 downstairs toilet

- Garage at end of garden – large garden at the back, small one at the front

- Would like to swap in August for similar type of house by the seaside, preferably in the south of France.

Useful vocabulary:
échanger – to swap
de préférence – preferably

Nantes, le 8 mars

Cher Matthew,

Je vais te parler de mon lycée. Il est mixte et compte douze cents élèves de onze à dix huit ans. Les cours commencent à huit heures du matin et finissent à cinq heures de l'après-midi.

Comme j'habite plutôt loin du lycée, je suis demi-pensionnaire. Je ne m'en plains pas. La nourriture est assez bonne en général.

Cette année, je suis en troisième et le travail marche bien. Normalement, je devrais passer en seconde sans problème l'année prochaine.

J'aimerais bien que tu me parles de ton école. Est-elle mixte? Combien d'élèves y a-t-il? Ils ont quel âge? Quelles sont les matières que tu étudies? Lesquelles préfères-tu? Quels jours de la semaine travailles-tu? Tu es demi-pensionnaire? En quelle classe es-tu? C'est vrai que les Anglais doivent porter un uniforme scolaire? Comment est le tien? Tu peux m'envoyer une photo de toi?
Écris bientôt.
Amitiés
Luc

2 Write an account of approximately 100 words in French of what Marc did this morning. Use the suggestions below and continue the story using your own imagination.

réveillé – levé – lavé – descendu – pris le petit déjeuner – préparé son cartable – embrassé sa mère – attendu l'autobus – arrivé à l'école – (imaginez la suite!)

3 Your friend Luc is telling you about his school and asking you about yours. Read his letter.

Now write a reply in French of approximately 100 words.

FINDING YOUR WAY

2 BASIC Listening

1 You will hear four people asking a policeman the way to various places, and the replies. After each question and answer, which you will hear twice, write down which letter on the map corresponds to each place.

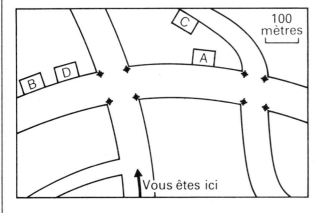

Vous êtes ici

100 mètres

2 You will hear five people explaining where various places are. Listen carefully to the tape. You will hear each section twice, then answer the questions below.

Section 1
Where exactly is the lost property office?

Section 2
Where exactly are the toilets?

Section 3
Where exactly is the disco?

Section 4
Where exactly is the tourist information office?

Section 5
To get to the beach, what you must you do (a, b or c)?
a) go past the police station, the church and turn right
b) go past the police station, turn right and go past the church
c) go past the police station, turn left and go past the church

3 Jacqueline, Michel and Peter are discussing what they want to do tonight. Peter is Michel's exchange partner and does not know the town very well. Listen carefully to their conversation, which is in two sections. You will hear each section twice. Read the questions before the tape starts.

Section 1
1 What will Jacqueline do tonight?
2 Why does Michel suggest a different outing?
3 What will Michel and Peter do

Section 2
4 Where is the leisure centre in relation to the hospital?
5 When and where do the two boys agree to meet?
6 Where is the café where the three agree to meet later?
7 Why is Jacqueline likely to be late meeting the two boys?

Now listen to the conversation again and choose the correct French equivalent to the following phrases:

8 open all day
   a) ouverte tous les jours
   b) ouverte tout le jour
9 do as you please
   a) fais ce que tu veux
   b) fais ce que tu peux
10 does that suit you?
   a) ça tu va?
   b) ça te va?
11 see you later
   a) plus tard
   b) à plus tard

1

Your penfriend, Pierre, who is a little older than you, is having his second driving lesson today. You have decided to go with him. See if you would have understood the instructions given by the driving instructor. You will hear each section of the passage twice. Read the questions before the tape starts.

Section 1

1 The driving instructor asked Pierre two questions. Give the meaning of one of them.

2 Before moving off, Pierre was told to do six different things. Here is a list of what he had to do. Note down the letters of the instructions in the order in which he had to do them.

A Look behind him
B Adjust his mirror
C Adjust his seat
D Start the engine
E Fasten his safety belt
F Use the indicator

Section 2

3 Where was Pierre told to stop the car exactly?

4 Pierre made a bad driving mistake. What was it?

5 What was his excuse?

Section 3

6 Draw a plan similar to the one below in your exercise book and show the route followed by Pierre in this section.

7 Why did Pierre refuse to obey one of the instructions?

Pierre est ici

2

Les Bâteaux-Mouches are boats in Paris that take visitors on the River Seine. As the river runs through the heart of Paris, visitors can get a glimpse of most places of interest from the *Bâteaux-Mouches*. The guide's commentary has been divided into two sections. You will hear each section twice. Read the instructions below carefully before the tape starts.

Copy the plan of the river below, and look at the boxes containing numbers and names of places on or near the Seine. As you listen to the tape, mark the number of each place mentioned in the commentary in the right place on the plan.

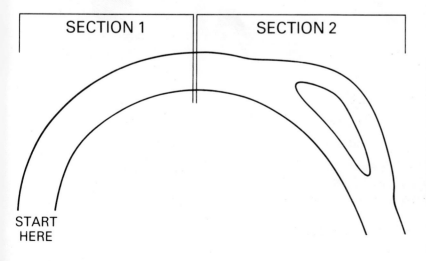

SECTION 1   SECTION 2

START HERE

Section 1
1 Pont Mirabeau
2 Maison de la radio et de la télévision
3 Notre-Dame de Grace
4 Tour Eiffel
5 Palais de Chaillot
6 Pont d'Iéna
7 Musée d'Art Moderne
8 Le Grand Palais
9 Eglise de la Madeleine
10 Les Invalides

Section 2
11 Jardin des Tuileries
12 Le Carrousel
13 Le Louvre
14 L'Ile de la Cité
15 Cathédrale Notre-Dame
16 Palais de Justice
17 Hôtel de Ville

2
BASIC
Speaking

1 One of you is a British visitor asking the way in a French town. The other is a resident replying. The three parts are in increasing order of difficulty for the resident: in the third section he/she has to make up his/her own replies.

Section 1

VISITOR	RESIDENT
Ask a passer-by the way to the tourist office.	C'est sur la place du marché.
Say you do not know where the market place is.	Prenez la première à gauche puis la deuxième à droite.
Ask how far it is.	A cinq minutes de marche.
Thank the passer-by and say goodbye.	Au revoir Monsieur.

Section 2

VISITOR	RESIDENT
Stop a passer-by and ask if the town centre is far.	Say it is about 3 kilometres away.
Ask whether there is a bus for the town centre.	Say yes, number 17.
Ask how frequent buses are and where the bus stop is.	Say every 15 minutes. The bus stop is 100 metres away on your right.
Thank the passer-by and say goodbye.	Say you are welcome and say goodbye.

Section 3

VISITOR	RESIDENT
Ask a passer-by if there is a post office nearby.	Reply suitably.
Ask how to get there.	
Repeat the information you have just been given.	
Say thank you and goodbye.	

2 Study the advertisement below and answer the questions.

1 Comment s'appelle l'hôtel-restaurant?
2 De quel village est-ce qu'il est près?
3 Donnez les directions pour aller à l'hôtel-restaurant. Vous partez de Chateauneuf-du-pape.

Le Logis d'Arnavel
HOTEL-RESTAURANT
Route de Roquemaure (à 3 km. du village sur la droite) - À CHATEAUNEUF-DU-PAPE
La nouvelle propriétaire, accompagnée d'une équipe jeune et très qualifiée, sera
heureuse de vous accueillir dans son logis en cette période de fêtes.

1 Study the street plan of Boulogne. Work in pairs, and take turns to ask each other the way to different places, from the Gendarmerie. Give each other detailed instructions.

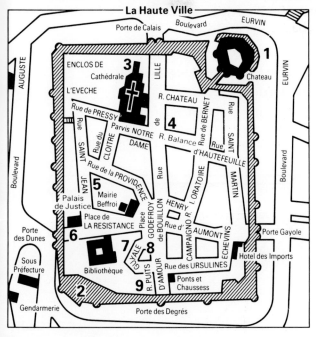

Example:

A Pardon, Monsieur, pour aller au château, s'il vous plaît?

B Passez la porte des Dunes et continuez sur le boulevard Auguste. Prenez la porte de Calais à droite et vous arrivez dans la rue de Lille. Prenez la première à gauche et l'entrée du château est sur votre gauche.

Now ask each other the way to:

1 the library
2 the cathedral
3 the town hall
4 the law courts
5 the 'hôtel des impôts'

2 Work in pairs. The plan below shows the position of vehicles just before an accident took place. Take it in turns to ask and answer the questions, using the plan.

1 D'où la voiture venait-elle?

2 Dans quelle direction allait le camion?

3 Qu'est-ce qui vous fait croire que l'autobus allait dans la direction de Lyon, et non pas vers le centre ville, par exemple?

4 Quel véhicule avait signalé son intention de se diriger vers le centre ville?

5 Pourquoi le camion avait-il choisi la route Nationale 7 et non pas la route Nationale 5?

6 Si la camionnette voulait aller en ville, quelles directions devait-elle prendre?

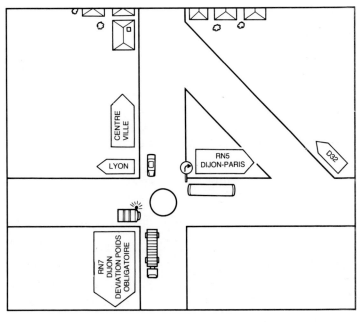

1 True or false? Study the map below.

1 Le cinéma est à côté du supermarché.

2 La statue est au milieu de la place.

3 L'église est près de la mairie.

4 L'épicerie est en face de la charcuterie.

5 La poste est entre l'épicerie et le supermarché.

6 La voiture est derrière le cycliste.

7 Le syndicat d'initiative est loin de la mairie.

8 L'arrêt d'autobus est tout près du théâtre.

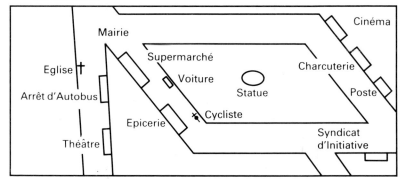

2 Read the letter that Martine's mother sent. She gives an account of an excursion she really enjoyed. With the help of the map above, sketch out the route Martine's parents took.

Carpentras, le 3 août

Chère Martine,

Je vais te raconter l'excursion qu'on a faite hier. C'était fantastique! On est partis de Carpentras sur la route D950, et après avoir passé Sarrians, on a tourné à droite, car on nous avait dit qu'il n'y avait rien de spécial à voir à Jonquières. On a donc passé quatre jolis villages avant de prendre à gauche pour arriver à Vaison-la-Romaine! En effet, ce n'était pas la peine d'allonger l'excursion pour passer à Entrechaux. La route, d'ailleurs, n'est pas très bonne dans cette direction. Ensuite, on s'est dirigé vers Villedieu et avons dû changer de route car ton père voulait absolument déguster les vins de Rasteau. Comme il commençait à se faire tard, on a décidé de rentrer par le plus court chemin. On a donc manqué de jolis villages comme Courthézon par exemple, mais on est arrivés à Carpentras à temps pour le dîner. Quelle bonne journée!

Je t'embrasse Maman

Read this letter carefully and then answer the questions.

Rouen le 27 août.

Cher John,

Ça va? Écoute, avec le nombre de touristes qu'on a en ce moment, au syndicat d'initiative, ils m'ont dit qu'ils n'ont plus de plans de la ville. Je vais faire de mon mieux pour t'expliquer ce qu'il faut faire pour me trouver. Surtout, ne prends pas de taxi, ils coûtent un prix fou!

Bon, en sortant de la gare, prends tout de suite à gauche dans la Rue Contrescarpe. Passe la gendarmerie que tu verras sur ta droite en face du café des Arts et tourne à droite. Ne vas pas jusqu'à la gare routière qui est au bout de la rue, mais tourne à gauche aux premiers feux. Tu es dans la rue de la République maintenant. Le lycée est sur ta gauche près l'hôtel de ville. Entre les deux, il y a une petite rue dont j'ai oublié le nom. Prends la. Juste avant le cinéma, sur ta droite, prends à droite et tu es dans la bonne rue. C'est le numéro vingt-huit. J'espère que tu t'y retrouveras.

Donne-moi un coup de fil avant d'arriver.

Amicalement

Alain

1 Why didn't Alain send John a plan of the town?

2 Why did he recommend John not to take a taxi?

3 At the end of his letter, what did Alain ask John to do before his arrival?

4 Using the information given in the letter, draw a plan of the route John will have to follow to get to his penfriend's house. Write as many details as you can on your plan.

2 BASIC Writing

1 You are camping at the seaside, on holiday with your parents. You wish to send a postcard to your penfriend that shows the beach and as much of the town as possible. You finally find one that you like. It shows the beach in the foreground with the promenade and its many hotels, restaurants and shops. In the background are the church and the town hall, and still further away the campsite and the castle. Draw the outline of a postcard in your exercise book and write a message of about 50 words explaining how you can walk from the beach to the campsite each day. Make up a French address.

2 *La chasse au trésor.*

As she knows that you are good in French, your French teacher, who is organising a treasure hunt for younger pupils, has asked you to write in French the messages that will lead the youngsters to the treasure. Your teacher has given you a map on which she has placed the spots where your messages are to be hidden. Write simple messages that will help the youngsters to find the treasure.

3 Your teacher has asked for suggestions from the class for the activities of a party of French pupils coming on an exchange visit. He asks each of you to make up a programme for one day, covering meeting places, activities and method of transport. Copy the table below and fill it in.

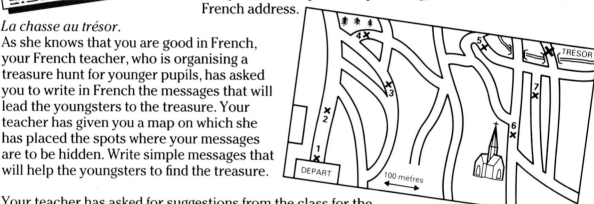

L'heure	Où on se rencontre	Pour aller où?	Comment?
9.30	devant la gare routière	à la cathédrale	à pied
10.30			
12.00			
1.30			
3.00			
6.00			

1 Your French penfriend has already asked you if it will be possible for him/her to visit you with his/her parents next month. As you live in a newly-built area, there is little point in sending a map of the town. Write a letter in French of about 100 words that includes the following points:

- Acknowledge his/her letter.
- Confirm that you and your parents will be happy to welcome them to your house.
- Directions to get to your house:
  a) leave the motorway at exit 15
  b) follow the signs to the town centre
  c) at the second set of traffic lights, turn left
  d) go straight on until you get to the church
  e) turn right after the church and go over the bridge
  f) your house is 100 metres after the bridge on the left
- Ask the likely date and time of their arrival.
- Say you look forward to their visit

2 Your penfriend is planning to pay you a short visit and is interested to know more about your town. Read his letter first, then write a reply in French (80 to 100 words). Make sure you answer all the questions he has asked you!

Calais, le 5 avril

Cher Andrew,

Je te remercie de ta lettre qui m'a bien fait plaisir. J'aimerais que tu me parles de ta ville. Il y a un cinéma ? Il est loin de chez toi ? Vous avez un centre de loisirs ? Est-ce qu'il est en dehors de la ville ? Ici, on n'a pas toutes les facilités qu'on aimerait avoir parce que la ville n'est pas très grande.

Et ton école, à quelle distance est-elle de chez toi ? Tu y vas à pied ? Moi, il faut que je prenne le car, c'est plutôt loin. Un jour, je voudrais venir te voir, juste pour la journée, et j'arriverai par le train. Tu peux me donner les directions de la gare à chez toi ? Ce sera une visite surprise comme ça ! A bientôt donc

Amicalement

Bernard

3 BASIC Listening

SHOPPING

1 Listen carefully to these three shop announcements. You will hear each announcement twice. Then answer the questions below.

Section 1

Describe Daniel.
Where can he be collected?

Section 2

At what time will the shop close next Saturday?

Section 3

Copy this table and complete it.

	What is reduced?	In which department is it?	On which floor is it?
1			
2			
3			
4			

2 Listen carefully to the five following advertisements, recorded from French radio. Each advertisement will be heard twice. Then answer the questions below.

Advertisement 1

In how many forms is the product advertised here presented?

Name two of these forms.

Advertisement 2

What do the Galeries Barbès offer in this advertisement?

Advertisement 3

What does Citroën offer its customers?

Advertisement 4

What particular produce is on offer at Intermarché?

How much does a 2½ kg packet cost?

Advertisement 5

Name the newspaper advertised here.

Name one of the articles to be found in it this week.

```
        BOOTS THE CHEMISTS LTD
             (LANDSIDE)
NIT 5, THE VILLAGE,  SOUTH TERMINAL
        TEL NO: (01293) 568060


NSON & JOHNSON                1.75
ANG MED RED T/B               1.45
 TOTAL                        3.20

 CASH                         3.20


PREVIOUS POINTS TOTAL         1036
OINTS AWARDED                   13
EW POINTS TOTAL               1049


  3919 1076 001          054314460
E: 16/02/00            TIME:  8:54

     THANK YOU FOR SHOPPING
           AT BOOTS
```

worry about changing your mind.
happy to exchange or refund
with receipt or proof of

n't have proof of purchase, we
lace or give Boots Gift Vouchers
uivalent value.

the safety of our customers, we
nnot accept returned medicines,
cosmetics and food, unless faulty.

This does not affect your statutory rights.

Boots welcomes comments from its
customers. If you would like to contact
us, please ring 08450 70 80 90 (local
rate) and we would be happy to listen
and help.

1 Thane Road West
Nottingham NG2 3AA
Reg VAT No. 116300129

 Paper made from
100% recycled fibre

    Official Health and Beauty Retailer

Please retain this receipt

Don't worry about changing your mind.
Boots is happy to exchange or refund
purchases with receipt or proof of
purchase.

If you don't have proof of purchase, we

1

Listen carefully to the four following commercials recorded from French radio. Each advertisement will be heard twice. Then answer the questions below.

Advertisement 1

Name two things that can be bought at Castorama.

Advertisement 2

Justify the name of the magazine advertised here.

Advertisement 3

What does Euromarché advertise here?

What do they call it in French and when will it end?

Advertisement 4

Here, Galeries Barbès are advertising payment facilities for their customers. Give more details about this offer.

2

Peter is in France buying trousers. Listen carefully to the conversation he has with the shopkeeper. You will hear it twice. Then answer the questions below.

Section 1

1. How much do the trousers in which Peter is interested cost?
2. For what colour does he ask?
3. What size is he, do you think?

Section 2

4. How does Peter justify to the shopkeeper his asking for a discount?
5. Under what condition is the shopkeeper prepared to give Peter a discount?
6. What is the size of that discount?
7. What two other things does Peter ask the shopkeeper to do?
8. Who is Monsieur Roulin?
9. How much does Peter pay altogether?

3 BASIC Speaking

Paired work.

a) *A la boulangerie.*

SHOPPER	ASSISTANT
Greet the assistant.	Greet the shopper.
Ask for two French sticks.	Give the shopper what he/she asked for; ask if there is anything else.
Say that is all you need. Ask how much you owe.	Answer the shopper's question.
Pay and leave.	

b) *A l'épicerie.*

SHOPPER	ASSISTANT
Greet the assistant.	Greet the shopper.
Ask for a quantity (make it up) of cheese.	Give the shopper what he/she asked for. Ask if there is anything else.
Ask the price of ham.	Answer the shopper's question (make up a price per 100 g).
Ask for four slices.	Give the shopper what he/she asked for. Ask if there is anything else.
Say no, and ask how much you owe altogether.	Say the price is 18F50.
Give a 20 franc note.	Give the shopper the correct change.
Count your change, and say goodbye.	Say goodbye.

c) *Au magasin de chaussures.*

SHOPPER	ASSISTANT
Greet the shop assistant.	Greet the shopper.
Say you would like to try the red shoes you saw in the window.	Ask what size the shopper takes.
Tell the assistant your size.	Bring the shoes. Ask if they are satisfactory.
Ask what other colours are available.	Answer the question (make up the other colours).
Say that you would like them in black.	Say your shop does not have these shoes in black.
Ask if another shop has them in black.	Make up an answer.

1 Répondez aux questions.

1 Qui fait les achats chez vous?

2 Est-ce que vous les faites? Pourquoi (pas)?

3 Comment dépensez-vous votre argent de poche?

4 Où se trouve l'épicerie dans votre ville/ village?
la boucherie?
la boulangerie?

5 Quels sont les magasins où votre famille va pour acheter à manger?

6 Vous préférez les supermarchés ou les petits magasins? Pourquoi?

7 A quelle distance de chez vous y a-t-il un supermarché? Comment s'appelle-t-il? Décrivez-le.

8 Qu'est-ce que vous achèteriez si vous aviez beaucoup d'argent?

2 Study the picture below, then answer the questions.

1 Qu'est-ce que l'enfant à gauche de l'image aimerait acheter?

2 Qu'est-ce que sa mère est en train d'acheter?

3 Décrivez ce que sa mère a dans son chariot.

4 Qu'est-ce qu'on peut acheter au rayon des légumes?

5 Pourquoi est-ce qu'il faut faire la queue au rayon des légumes?

6 Si vous avez besoin d'un produit pour faire la vaisselle, dans quel rayon le trouverez-vous?

7 Quels autres produits peut-on acheter à ce rayon?

8 Pourquoi l'homme qui achète du pâté n'a-t-il pas de chariot, pensez-vous?

9 Où doit-on payer tous ses achats?

10 Pourquoi est-ce que vous n'avez pas le droit de sortir par la porte à droite de l'image?

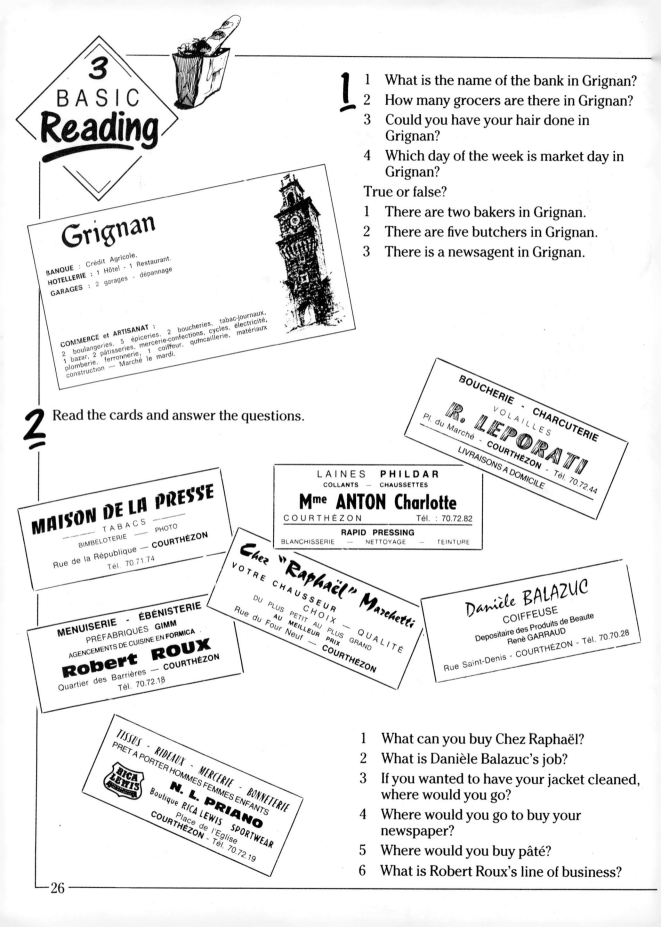

1

1 What is the name of the bank in Grignan?
2 How many grocers are there in Grignan?
3 Could you have your hair done in Grignan?
4 Which day of the week is market day in Grignan?

True or false?

1 There are two bakers in Grignan.
2 There are five butchers in Grignan.
3 There is a newsagent in Grignan.

Grignan

BANQUE : Crédit Agricole.
HOTELLERIE : 1 Hôtel - 1 Restaurant.
GARAGES : 2 garages - dépannage

COMMERCE et ARTISANAT :
2 boulangeries, 5 épiceries, 2 boucheries, tabac-journaux,
1 bazar, 2 pâtisseries, mercerie-confections, cycles, électricité,
plomberie, ferronnerie, 1 coiffeur, quincaillerie, matériaux
construction — Marché le mardi.

2 Read the cards and answer the questions.

BOUCHERIE - CHARCUTERIE
VOLAILLES
R. LEPORATI
Pl. du Marché - COURTHÉZON - Tél. 70.72.44
LIVRAISONS A DOMICILE

MAISON DE LA PRESSE
TABACS
BIMBELOTERIE — PHOTO
Rue de la République — COURTHÉZON
Tél. 70.71.74

LAINES **PHILDAR**
COLLANTS — CHAUSSETTES
Mme ANTON Charlotte
COURTHÉZON   Tél. : 70.72.82
RAPID PRESSING
BLANCHISSERIE — NETTOYAGE — TEINTURE

Chez "Raphaël" Marchetti
VOTRE CHAUSSEUR
CHOIX — QUALITÉ
DU PLUS PETIT AU PLUS GRAND
AU MEILLEUR PRIX
Rue du Four Neuf — COURTHÉZON

Danièle BALAZUC
COIFFEUSE
Depositaire des Produits de Beaute
Renè GARRAUD
Rue Saint-Denis - COURTHÉZON - Tél. 70.70.28

MENUISERIE - ÉBÉNISTERIE
PRÉFABRIQUÉS GIMM
AGENCEMENTS DE CUISINE EN FORMICA
Robert ROUX
Quartier des Barrières — COURTHÉZON
Tél. 70.72.18

TISSUS - RIDEAUX - MERCERIE - BONNETERIE
PRET A PORTER HOMMES FEMMES ENFANTS
N. L. PRIANO
Boutique RICA LEWIS SPORTWEAR
Place de l'Eglise
COURTHÉZON - Tél. 70.72.19

1 What can you buy Chez Raphaël?
2 What is Danièle Balazuc's job?
3 If you wanted to have your jacket cleaned, where would you go?
4 Where would you go to buy your newspaper?
5 Where would you buy pâté?
6 What is Robert Roux's line of business?

3
1 Give the address of the supermarket.
2 Which two features of Intermarché are highlighted in these advertisements?

INTERMARCHÉ
Les Mousquetaires de la distribution
à 200 mètres
ROUTE DE NANTES · SENÉ - VANNES

INTERMARCHÉ :
LES PRIX -
LA QUALITÉ

INTERMARCHÉ :
DES PRIX BAS TOUTE L'ANNÉE
EN TOUTES SAISONS
EN TOUS LIEUX

4
Study the bill below.
1 Madame Leblanc bought some liver pâté. How much did she pay for it?
2 How many items did she purchase from the fruit and vegetables counter?
3 How much did she have to pay altogether?

```
    MERCI DE VOTRE
  VISITE * A BIENTOT *
   02-06-84 ₦130000
      6      ₃1.30
  16928 EauSM
   083 CHARCUT     7.80
   084 FR.LEG.    20.20
   084 FR.LFG.    11.80
   079 CREMERI    10.55
    751 BAGET      9.60
   079 CREMERI     1.85
    713 CAMPr     10.30
    713 CAMPr      7.10
   084 FR.LFG.     7.10
   079 CREMERI     4.18
   079 CREMERI     6.13
   039 ENTRETI     7.13
   039 ENTRETI    11.95
    410 COCAL   ₁₄ 6.35
   299+CONSI      3.40
   069 EPICERI     2.00
   069 EPICERI     4.15
  S/TOTAL         4.15
                135.74
  ESPECES
  RENDU         150.00
       14.26
```

**L'INDICATEUR
INTERMARCHÉ**

A INTERMARCHÉ, nous sommes immunisés
contre l'épidémie.

LES MOUSQUETAIRES

S O M M A I R E

5
Above is the index of a booklet that gives the prices of all the products sold at Intermarché.

To which page would you turn if you wanted to know the price of:

a) cakes   f) cat food
b) chocolate   g) mineral water
c) sweets   h) shampoo
d) milk   i) washing-up liquid
e) jam

How long is the average French family's holiday?

AH! LES VACANCES!

Du soleil sur la peau, quelques cartes postales pour dire aux amis que tout va bien.
On oublie tout pendant un mois et on a raison car on se sent bien.

un petit bonjour de la Mer, temps pas trop mauvais Bronze, bien!! gros bisous à tous.
Sophie

M. Edouard d'Aymar
3 rue des Tonnyers
LA Rochelle
17 OC2

MAIS DUR, DUR, DUR LA RENTREE.

Mais le retour des vacances, c'est aussi le retour brutal à la vie quotidienne et lorsque vous ouvrirez votre boîte aux lettres, les mauvaises surprises vont commencer…

What is likely to spoil the fun when the family returns?
What is the content of the mail as depicted in this advertisement?

LA PUBLICITÉ ANNONCE LES DÉPENSES

Même la publicité que vous trouverez en arrivant vous rappellera :
• Qu'il faut penser aux fournitures scolaires
• Qu'il faut équiper les enfants pour l'hiver
• Qu'il faut reconstituer les provisions de base.
Alors, au revoir les vacances, bonjour la rentrée !
Heureusement, INTERMARCHÉ pense à vous.

What are the main concerns of the average family on their return from a summer holiday?

POUR S'EN SORTIR A LA RENTRÉE: INTERMARCHÉ

A INTERMARCHÉ, nous ne sommes pas magiciens. Nous ne prétendons pas vous offrir l'éponge qui effacera l'ardoise de la rentrée ! Mais les Mousquetaires ont uni leurs efforts, une fois encore, pour que l'addition soit moins "salée" et dans tous les secteurs... En alimentaire... comme en fournitures scolaires !

Intermarché claim they can help. How and to what extent?

PROFITEZ DE VOS VACANCES,... A LA RENTRÉE, INTERMARCHÉ SERA A VOS COTÉS!

Alors, profitez du soleil d'août, surtout si vous êtes en vacances !
Et soyez confiants.
• Vous savez que les prix bas de cet indicateur sont valables jusqu'à fin août, pas de mauvaises surprises !
• Vous savez que début septembre, un autre indicateur paraîtra comme chaque mois, avec encore 500 prix bas pour mieux passer la rentrée.

L'INDICATEUR INTERMARCHÉ: 500 PRIX PARMI LES PLUS BAS DU MARCHÉ

The *indicateur* presented here is supposed to help you enjoy your holiday.
What is it? How often is the *indicateur* published?

3 BASIC Writing

1 It is nearly the end of your exchange visit. You have had a wonderful time and would like to give a present to every person in Marc's family. After careful thinking, you have decided what to buy each person. Here are the notes you have made:

Marc's dad smokes. He also likes fishing.
Marc's mum likes reading and gardening.
Jean-Louis likes toys and games.
Michèle like fashionable clothes.
Marc likes going out.

Now write in your diary in French the shopping list you used to buy your presents. Copy and complete the list below.

CADEAUX POUR LA FAMILLE

pour le père de Marc: ....

pour la mère de Marc: ....

pour Jean-Louis: ....

pour Michèle: ....

pour Marc: ....

2 Write a letter in French of about 80 words to your penfriend Philippe, making the following points:

– Thank Philippe for the present he has just sent you.
– Say what you are buying for your family and friends for Christmas.
– Say where you bought each item.
– Say to Philippe that you are sending him a present in a parcel today.
– Say what it is and where you bought it, and say that you hope he will like it.
– Wish him and his family a Happy Christmas.

The camera you bought in France last month is already broken!
Write a letter in French of about 100 words to the
manufacturer: Bijou France, 3 rue de la République, Avignon
84000, making the following points:

– Say when and where you bought the
camera.
– Say that you have kept the receipt
(attached to this letter).
– Say that your camera failed last time you
wanted to take a picture.
– Explain that you have taken your camera
to a repairer in England but that he could
not do anything for you.
– Complain about the quality of the
manufacturer's products.
– Demand your money back or for the
camera to be repaired by the
manufacturer.
– Thank the manufacturer in advance for his
services.

Study the pictures below and relate the story in French.

1 You will hear a conversation at the café where someone is buying an ice-cream. Which flavour does he choose? You will hear the conversation twice.

2 You will hear a conversation between a teenager and a waiter. At the end of the conversation, the teenager buys a particular sandwich. What sort of sandwich does she buy? You will hear the conversation twice.

3 You will hear a conversation between two friends. At the end of the conversation, one calls the waiter and is ready to order. What does she order? You will hear the conversation twice.

4 French people are generally thought to be keen on food. Our interviewer went out to find out what type of food and drink they are particularly fond of. You will hear one of his interviews twice. Copy this form into your notebook and complete it.

```
                   INTERVIEW NOTES

Mr/Mrs/Miss ?

Age ..............................................

Number of meals per day .........................

Favourite cold drink ............................

Favourite hot drink .............................

Favourite food ..................................

Favourite fruit .................................

Favourite vegetable .............................

Favourite meat ..................................

Are you a vegetarian? ...........................
```

1 You are staying in Brittany with your French penfriend and she takes you to the *crêperie* owned by her uncle. You greatly enjoy a *crêpe au jambon* and ask your friend's uncle for the recipe. You note down what he tells you, but find later that some details are missing. You telephone him and he reads the complete recipe to you. You will hear the recipe twice. Make a summary of the recipe like this one, and then complete it by listening to the tape.

1. The Batter:	2. The filling:	3. Mix the ingredients for the batter in a bowl and leave for ____ minutes.
125g: _____	_____ butter	4. Cook the mushrooms for ____ minutes.
Tablespoon of _____	_____ flour	
1 _____	_____ mushrooms	5. Put _____ in each pancake.
1 glass of _____	_____ ham	6. Last stage of cooking:
A little _____	salt, pepper	_____

2 Two French people in a restaurant are discussing which meal to choose. Listen carefully to their conversation, then decide which meal each of them chooses.

3 On holiday with your parents in France, you are listening to the local radio station. This morning, the representative of the *Guide Michelin* is being interviewed on local restaurants. As his advice could be very useful to you and your parents, you listen very carefully. You will hear the interview twice, then answer the questions below.

1 The best restaurants are not necessarily expensive. True or false?

2 We are told that there are restaurants that are expensive for reasons other than the quality of the meals they provide. Give two such reasons.

3 If what you want is good food that is not too expensive, where are you advised to look?

4 What kind of wine is often recommended to customers?

5 How is family cooking defined in this programme?

6 Why are such restaurants often inexpensive?

Menu du Jour
60 francs
Crudités
Poulet Marengo
Pommes sautées
Fromage
Dessert
Vin en sus

Menu Gastronomique
140 francs
Crudités
Truite
Biftek
Légumes
Fromage
Dessert
Vin compris

Menu Touristique
80 francs
Charcuterie du pays
Boeuf Strogonoff
Légumes
Fromage
Dessert
Vin compris

La Carte
Pâté 79 f
Huîtres 30f
Sole 45 f
Tournedos 50f
Côte d'agneau 55f
Fromage 15f
Glaces 18f

4
BASIC
Speaking

1 Work in pairs. One of you is the customer,
the other the waiter in a café.

WAITER

Greet the customer and ask what he/she
would like.

Give your customer the bill, saying the total
price (16 F 50) aloud.

Thank the customer.

CUSTOMER

Say you will have a Coke. Say you would also
like a ham sandwich. Ask for the bill.

Pay what you owe. Remember to leave a tip
(tell the waiter you have left one).

2 Work in pairs. One of you is the customer at the restaurant, the other is the waiter.

WAITER

Bonjour. Vous voudriez une table pour
combien de personnes?

Vous désirez prendre un apéritif?

Etes-vous prêt à passer votre commande?

Quelle sorte de vin voulez-vous?

Que désirez-vous comme entrée?

Et comme viande?

Quels légumes aimeriez-vous?

Vous prendrez du fromage ou un dessert?

Vous voulez un café pour finir?

Merci. Bon appétit.

CUSTOMER

Say it is for two people.

Say yes and order something suitable.

Say yes, you would like the menu at 80 francs.

Say red.

Order pâté.

Order steak.

Order a green salad.

Say you will have cheese.

Order two black coffees.

3 Study the advertisement below and answer
the questions.

1 Ce restaurant est à quelle distance
d'Orange?
2 Ça ouvre à quelle heure le soir?
3 C'est ouvert pour le repas de midi?
4 Quel jour de la semaine est-ce que c'est
fermé?
5 Quelle est la spécialité du chef?
6 Pourquoi est-ce que le restaurant
s'appelle Chez Moustache?

A 3.500 km d'Orange. route de Châteauneuf. «le Grès»

Pizzéria ..... Restaurant
«CHEZ MOUSTACHE»

Cadre champêtre - Ambiance - 3 salles
Repas sur commande
Ouvert tous les soirs à partir de 19 h et le dimanche à midi
Fermeture hebdomadaire le mardi - Tél. 90.34.31.03

1 Answer the questions below in French.

1 Est-ce que vous allez souvent dans un restaurant?

2 A quelle(s) occasion(s) y allez-vous?

3 Est-ce que vous pouvez recommander un restaurant qui est particulièrement bon? Justifiez votre réponse.

4 Quel est votre plat préféré?

5 Si vous allez au café avec des amis, qu'est-ce que vous prenez?

6 Quelles sont les différences entre les cafés français et les pubs?

7 Vous êtes déjà allé dans un pub?

8 Quel âge faut-il avoir pour avoir le droit d'entrer dans un pub?

9 A l'école, vous mangez à la cantine? Si oui, décrivez un repas typique.

10 Si vous rentrez chez vous à midi, qu'est-ce que vous mangez d'habitude?

11 Qui fait la cuisine chez vous?

12 Aimez-vous faire la cuisine? Pourquoi (pas)?

2 One of you is the customer, the other the waiter at a café.

WAITER	CUSTOMER
Greet the customer and ask what he/she would like.	Order a coffee.
Ask if they want a large or a small coffee, with or without sugar.	Answer the question.
Ask if that is all.	Say no and ask what sort of sandwiches they have.
Say pâté, ham, cheese, and say how much each costs.	Order a ham sandwich and ask for the bill.
Bring the bill and say that service is not included.	Pay the bill, adding 10% for the service.
Thank the customer.	

4 BASIC Reading

1

Study the menu carefully and then answer the questions.

1 What *entrée* could a vegetarian choose?

2 Could you eat a fish dish at this restaurant?

3 What would you order if you felt like beef?

4 What vegetables are on offer?

5 How much would a portion of local cheese cost you?

6 Are the prices quoted all inclusive?

~Carte~

NOS ENTREES ~
(Voir notre Carte ‹‹Mer‹‹)

— La Terrine Maison aux Foies de Volailles — 18.50
   (marbrée de Filet de Canard)
— Jambon Fumé du Pays — 16
— La Salade Niçoise (tomate, œuf dur, — 27.50
   anchoix, poivrons, haricots verts)
— Les Crêpes Jambon Paprika — 25
— Les Œufs en Cocotte à la Crème — 25

NOS POISSONS ~
(Consulter notre Carte ‹‹Mer››)

NOS VIANDES ~
— Les Côtes d'Agneau de Pré-Salé Grillés — 49
— Le Château Grillé Vert Pré — 54
— Le Château à l'échalote — 55
— Le Rognon de Veau Beaugé — 81
— Le Pigeon Braisé aux Petits Pois — 82
— L'Emincé de Magret de Canard au Cidre — 66
— Les Lichettes de Bœuf Cru au Jus de — 63
   Citron

NOS LÉGUMES ~
— Frites. Haricots Verts. Salades Vertes. Riz — 16

NOS FROMAGES ~
— Le Plateau de Fromages — 18
— Le Fromage Blanc du Pays — 13.60

Après 21 h 30, service en + 15%   PRIX NETS

2

Les Restaurants de la Semaine

BISTRO DE LA GARE Nouvelles suggestions, menu 37,50 F snc, les fameux aloyaux sur le gril, nouv. gde carte de desserts MICHEL OLIVER. Ouv. T.L.J. jusq. 1 h du matin. 30, rue Saint-Denis, 59, boulevard du Montparnasse, 2, rue de la Chaussée-d'Antin, 73, Champs-Élysées.

AU PIED DE COCHON Le fameux restaurant des Halles, 6, r. Coquillière. 236.11.75. **BANC D'HUITRES. OUVERT TOUTE** **OUVERT 24 H SUR 24** **L'ANNÉE.** Crustacé de vermeil. Ses viandes succul.

RUC UNIVERS 1, pl. Théâtre-Français (face Comédie-Française). 260.31.57. Poissons, fruits de mer. Déj., dîn., soup. T.l.j. Cadre nouveau.

L'EUROPÉEN Face gare de Lyon. 343.99.70. Tous les jours, 11 h à 2 h du matin. **BANC D'HUITRES, CHOUCR. ET CUISINE D'AUTREFOIS.**

TOUR D'ARGENT 6, pl. de la Bastille. 344.32.19 et 32.32. Tous les jours jusqu'à 1 h 15 du matin. Huîtres, coquillages, grillades.

TOUR DE LYON 1, rue de Lyon, face à la gare. 343.88.30. Poissons, huîtres, grillades. Tous les jours jusqu'à 1 h 15 du matin.

1 You only have 40 francs left. Name the restaurant where you can be sure of getting a meal with your money.

2 It is half past one in the morning. You are starving! Where can you go for a meal?

3 On which day of the week is this restaurant closed?

4 What sort of restaurant is this?

5 What can you buy to take away here?

allez aux escargots

Faites provision des meilleurs escargots de Paris cuits aux aromates et remplis de beurre frais extra-fin, à la
MAISON DE L'ESCARGOT
sauf le lundi, tous les jours jusqu'à 20 h, le dimanche de 9 à 13 h, 79, rue Fondary-15° - 575.31.09.

As your parents have planned to sample French cuisine, they have asked you to study the local paper that always advertises restaurants in this area. Study the newspaper cutting before answering the following questions.

1 Where is the restaurant Les Dunes in Audierne situated exactly?

2 At La Bagatelle in Concarneau, would you be served a meal at 1 am on Tuesday night?

3 What is the speciality of the restaurant called Le Marsouin?

4 Which restaurant specialises in fish dishes?

5 Name one restaurant where you can be sure of being served lunch every day of the week.

6 One of the restaurants also offers a disco. When is it open?

7 Name one restaurant that offers a takeaway service.

8 Which restaurant could you choose if you wanted to taste shellfish?

2 Read this recipe carefully and answer the following questions.

1 How many frogs' legs would you need for four people?

2 Name six different ingredients that make up the recipe.

● **AUDIERNE.** — Sur la plage, LES DUNES, rest. panoramique. Ses menus, sa carte, ses spécialités. Tél. 98.70.01.19. Ouvert tous les jours.

● **AUDIERNE.** — LE GLACIER, restaurant, route de la Pointe du Raz, ouvert sur réserv. pour banquets et repas de famille. Tél. 98.70.08.26. Françoise et Jean Donnart.

● **CHATEAULIN.** — L'AUBERGE DES DUCS DE LIN, dans son cadre de verdure, grillades sur braises de bois, feuilleté de sole au ris de veau, panaché de coquillages, brochettes de coquilles Saint-Jacques. Parking. Vue sur l'Aulne. Tél. 98.86.04.20.

● **CONCARNEAU.** — Ville Close, LA BAGATELLE, derrière remparts. Repas tardifs. Menus 55, 80, 130 F. Menus enfants 25 F. Service jusqu'à 1 heure du matin. Ouvert tous les jours sauf le mardi. Grand choix de vins. 12, rue Théophile-Louarn, 29110 Concarneau. Tél. 98.97.49.98.

● **MOUSTERLIN-FOUESNANT.** — Restaurant LE RÉCIF, près de la plage de Cleut-Rouz. Ouvert tous les week-ends. Repas de famille, mariages. Repas de groupe sur commande. Menus à 75 F, 100 F et 140 F. Tél. 98.56.06.45. Sa discothèque, le NASHVILLE, ouverte tous les soirs du mercredi au dimanche dès 22 h.

LE MARSOUIN vous accueille dans un cadre sympathique tous les vendredi, samedi, dimanche et jours fériés (en semaine sur commande). Spécialités de crêpes. Menus et grill à toute heure. Plats à emporter. Banquets, repas de famille. Prix modérés. Tél. 98.54.30.25.

● **PLONÉOUR-LANVERN.** — L'hôtel-restaurant des Voyageurs vous accueille dans un cadre agréable. Cuisine soignée. Sa cave. Nombreuses spécialités de poissons. Pour vos réserv. Tél. 98.87.61.35.

● **RIEC-SUR-BELON.** — AUBERGE DE KERLAND, sa table gourmande et l'assiette du pêcheur, dégustation de fruits de mer, dominant la vallée du Belon, route de Moëlan-sur-Mer, tél. 98.08.42.98. Réservations jusqu'à 21 h 30. Fermeture hebdomadaire dimanche soir et lundi midi.

● **QUIMPER.** — LE SAVOYARD. "Les sports d'hiver à Quimper". Restaurant de spécialités de Savoie. Charcuterie, hors d'œuvre, fromages, fondues des Alpes. Ouvert le midi et le soir jusqu'à minuit. 8, route de Douarnenez, Quimper. Tél. 98.53.67.21

Les Cuisses de Grenouilles Panées

Vous aurez besoin d'une demi-douzaine de cuisses par personne.

D'abord, préparez vos cuisses. Battez un œuf dans un bol, mettez-y sel et poivre et passez-y une a une vos cuisses de grenouilles. Enrobez ensuite vos cuisses de miettes de pain que vous aurez préparées à l'avance. Vous êtes maintenant prête à mettre vos cuisses à la poêle.

Faites chauffer un peu d'huile dans la poêle et mettez-y vos cuisses. Après trois ou quatre minutes, retournez-les. Quand elles sont prêtes, trois ou quatre minutes plus tard, versez un jus de citron dessus. Servez immédiatement.

Accompagnez votre plat de champignons de Paris et d'une salade verte.

4 BASIC Writing

1 It is your second day in France at your penfriend's. Yesterday, you experienced real French food for the first time. In your diary or notebook, make notes in French of what you ate.

RESTAURANT | LE GAULOIS

Mardi 8 Août

Le petit déjeuner ....
....

Le déjeuner ....
....
....

Le goûter ....
....

Le dîner ....
....
....

2 As it was your birthday yesterday, your parents treated you to a French meal in a restaurant. Write a postcard in French to your penfriend in which you tell him/her about your birthday and give details of the meal you had.

FROMAGE PUR 100% CHEVRE

houx-fleurs
KG
F
4,90

Brasserie Le Palace

* Omelettes — Jambon / Champignons / Fromage — 18 / 18 / 18

* Salades — Provençale / Camarguaise / Mexicaine / Taboulé / du Vigneron / du Pêcheur

* Pizzas — Anchois-Fromage / Jambon Fromage — 24 / 24

* Viandes (grillées-garnies) — Entrecôte / Côte de porc / Hamburger / Godiveaux / Baron d'agneau

It has been decided that you and your parents are going to Normandy between the 15th and 30th of June. Your parents have promised to take you to a French restaurant for your birthday (Monday 28th June). From the list of restaurants that you received from the local tourist office, you selected L'Auberge de L'Oasis, 3 rue de la plage, Montebourg. Write a letter of about 80 words in French to the restaurant, in which you make the following points:

— Explain that you will be on holiday in the area during the second fortnight in June.
— Ask which day of the week the restaurant is closed.
— If it is open on Mondays, ask if you can book a table for three people for 28th June.
— Ask the price of the set meals.
— Explain that it is a special treat for your birthday and say that you look forward to it.

Tell the story illustrated by the pictures below, in French.

ACCOMMODATION

1 A l'Auberge de Jeunesse

The warden of the youth hostel is telling you about the rules and regulations of the hostel. Listen to the warden carefully and answer the questions. You will hear each section twice.

Section 1

How can you show that you are a member of the Youth Hostels Association?

Section 2

At what time does the hostel close?

Section 3

At what time is breakfast? lunch? the evening meal?

Section 4

Which meals do you have to cook yourself?

Section 5

Why do you have to leave the hostel between 9 and 12?

Section 6

When are you expected to settle your bill?

Section 7

Give two examples of duties visitors are expected to perform.

2

Your parents want some more information about the hotel they have selected from a holiday brochure, and have asked you to phone. To your surprise, you hear information recorded on an answering machine. Listen to the tape, which will be played twice, and answer the questions.

Section 1

At what time of the year does the hotel open?

Section 2

How many rooms does the hotel have?

Section 3

Give the telephone number of the hotel.

Section 4

How much is it for a double room?

Section 5

Which animals are not welcome?

Section 6

Which meal does the hotel offer?

Section 7

How can you obtain more information?

Syndicat d'Initiative
Sous · Préfecture →
C.I.O.

Hôtels · Restaurants
Brasserie de la Place
Château de Montreuil
Darnétal le
France de

3

You are asking for information about a campsite over the phone. Copy the form then listen carefully and fill in the information you are given. You will hear the tape twice.

▽

Tent	. . . . . .	francs
Caravan	. . . . . .	francs
Car	. . . . . .	francs
Adults	. . . . . .	francs
Children	. . . . . .	francs
Shower	. . . . . .	francs

Other facilities:

. . . .

. . . .

. . . .

Listen carefully to these two ladies, who are each praising the hotels where they spent their last holiday: *Hôtel Mistral* and *Le Petit Nice*. You will hear each section twice, then decide which hotel you think *you* would prefer. Justify your answer. What did you not like about the other hotel?

You have decided to go to the tourist information office for advice on how to choose your hotel. In Section 1, you will hear the tourist office's advice. In Section 2, your father, who wants to try his French, books in at an hotel. You will hear his conversation with the hotel manager. In Section 3, your father is shown to the room by the hotel manager. You will hear the tape twice. Listen carefully and then answer the questions.

Section 1
1   What kind of hotels can you find near the beach?
2   What kind of hotels can you find in the town centre?

Section 2
3   Where exactly is the room which is offered?
4   How many people can stay there?
5   How long do you intend to stay in the hotel?
6   What does the hotel manager ask your father to do?

Section 3
7   What does your father think of the room?

5
BASIC
Speaking

1 Work in pairs. One of you is a camper arriving at a campsite with friends, the other is the receptionist at the site.

CAMPER	RECEPTIONIST
Greet the receptionist and ask if there is room at the campsite.	Ask what space is needed.
Say you have two small tents.	Ask for how long.
Say you want to stay for a week.	Ask how many people there are wanting to stay.
Say how many. Ask about the facilities.	Mention water, showers, toilets, etc.
Ask the price per night.	State a suitable price. Ask for the first night's fee.
Pay, thank the receptionist, and say goodbye.	

2 You will find this type of *relais* on the motorway. Study the advertisement and the key to the symbols then answer the questions.

1 Comment s'appelle cet hôtel?
2 Si vous voulez réserver une chambre, quel numéro devez-vous appeler?
3 Est-ce que c'est toujours ouvert?
4 Dans quelle ville se trouve cet hôtel?
5 Est-ce qu'on peut aussi y manger?
6 Les cartes de crédit sont-elles acceptées?
7 Il y a aussi un bureau de change. Qu'est-ce qu'on peut faire au bureau de change?
8 Qu'est-ce qu'il y a pour amuser les enfants?

Key
A Restaurant
B Hôtel
C Jeux d'enfants
D Carte de crédit
E Bureau de change
F Souterrain

Mâcon

A   B   C

D   E   F

Hotel Sofitel

(85) 33.19.00
Ouverture :
24 h sur 24

Answer the questions below in French.

1 Quand vous allez en vacances, d'habitude, faites-vous du camping, ou allez-vous à l'hôtel?

2 Est-ce que vous avez une tente? une caravane? Si oui, décrivez-la.

3 Vous préférez le camping ou l'hôtel? Expliquez vos raisons.

4 Si un hôtel a des étoiles, qu'est-ce que ça veut dire?

5 Si un hôtel fait pension/demi-pension, qu'est-ce que ça veut dire?

6 Comment fait-on pour réserver une chambre à l'hôtel?

7 Vous vous êtes déjà arrêté à une auberge de jeunesse? Si oui, décrivez dans quelles circonstances.

8 Etes-vous membre de l'Association des Auberges de Jeunesse?

9 Quels sont les avantages d'une auberge de jeunesse, pensez-vous?

10 Est-ce que vous avez votre propre chambre ou vous la partagez avec un frère ou une sœur? Qu'est-ce qu'il y a dans votre chambre? Vous y faites vos devoirs?

Study the picture below and answer the questions.

1 Expliquez ce que chaque personne dans la cuisine fait.

2 Qu'est-ce que les garçons qui descendent l'escalier portent sur le dos?

3 Comment savez-vous qu'il n'y a pas de places libres?

4 Quelle heure est-il? Selon vous, c'est le matin ou le soir? Donnez vos raisons.

5 Qu'est-ce que la jeune fille à la réception fait?

6 Si vous restez trois jours à cette auberge de jeunesse, combien cela vous coûtera-t-il?

7 Comment savez-vous qu'on est à l'intérieur d'une auberge de jeunesse et non pas d'un hôtel?

8 Qu'est-ce qui arrive aux trois garçons au milieu de l'escalier?

1

You have heard a lot about Pau and would like to book a room for you and your parents there. Which of these two hotels would you contact? Justify your choice.

HOTEL DE GRAMONT
★ ★ ★
Nouvelles Normes

Sur la plus belle place de PAU, au cœur du vieux quartier
Près du Château
3, place Gramont
PAU
Tél. (59) 27.84.04

HOTEL "LE PALAIS"
.. NN

18/20 rue Montpensier
64000 PAU
Tél. (59) 02.29.22
(4 lignes Groupees)
Telex FIC 541.249

★ Hotels Centre-ville
★ Chambres équipees de salle de bains - W.C. ligne téléphonique directe vers l'exterieur.
★ Salon télévision couleur.
★ Conditions pour séjour, V.R.P., Sociétes.

VILLE DE SAINTE-ANNE-D'AURAY (Morbihan)

CAMPING MUNICIPAL DU MOTTEN

Téléphone (97) 57.60.27

N° 298 FICHE de CONTROLE

Séjour de M SHARWOOD

du 27.09.87 inclus au 28.09.87

N° de Véhicule 1V

CATEGORIE	QUANTITÉ	PRIX UNITAIRE	TOTAL PAR JOUR	NOMBRE de JOURS	MONTANT
CAMPEURS Gdes personnes	2	2,80	5,60		
Enfant à 1,2 tarif					
Voitures	1	1,50	1,50		
Deux roues					
Emplacements	1	1,50	1,50		
			8,60	1	8,60
Electricité					
Eau chaude	2	0,70	1,40	1	1,40
Douches	4	1,00	4,00	1	4,00
				REÇU	14,00

◁ 2

This is the bill the Sharwoods were given after stopping at the Camping Municipal du Motten.

1 Where is the campsite situated?
2 How many days did the Sharwoods stay at the campsite?
3 How much does it cost to have a shower?
4 What was the charge per person per day?
5 What was the daily charge for pitching their tent?

L'AUBERGE DE LA JEUNESSE D'ORLEANS

Située à deux pas du centre ville, vous offre:
– une ambiance très familiale,
– un jardin pour se détendre,
– des bicyclettes pour les promenades.
– des activités touristiques.
– des stages.

▷ 3

True or false?

1 The youth hostel is a long way from the town centre.
2 The youth hostel has one dining room, one kitchen and 54 beds in dormitories.
3 Breakfast and lunch are served but you have to prepare the evening meal yourself.
4 There is a garden where you can relax.
5 The youth hostel is open from 10 am to 10 pm.

ET AUSSIE...
– 54 lits en chambres collectives,
– des douches,
– une salle à manger,
– une cuisine (les déjeuners et diners sont à préparer soi-même),
– des petits-déjeuners servis.

L'auberge est ouverte de 10 h à 22 heures.

Your penfriend, who lives in Coutances, has invited you and your family to spend a few days at Christmas. However, it is impossible to put up all the family, and he/she has sent you a list of hotels in Coutances. Your parents would like a hotel that offers meals, but they also want to keep the cost of the holiday to a minimum. A parking space will be needed for the car. Study the extract from the brochure. The key to abbreviations is given below.

Which hotel would you advise your parents to ring to make a reservation?

Key

hab. = *habitants*
OT = *office de tourisme*
SI = *syndicat d'initiative*
ch. = *chambres*
petit déj. = *petit déjeuner*
½p = *demi-pension*
P = *pension*
TA. = *toute l'année*
tél. ds les ch. = *téléphone dans les chambres*
Ag = *agence de voyage*
h = *heures*
quinz. = *quinzaine*

B3 50200 COUTANCES – *13439 hab.* - OT/SI - ☎ (33) 45.17.79
Cité episcopale - Cathédrale XIe-XIIIe - Eglise Saint-Nicolas XIIIe - Eglise Saint-Pierre XVe - Jardin public - Musée - Piscine - La plage est à 13 km - Paris : 330 km - Cherbourg: 75 km - Saint-Lô : 27 km - Avranches : 47 km.

** **GRAND HOTEL** - Place de la Gare - ☎ 45.06.55 - LOGIS DE FRANCE 25 ch.: 85/165 F - Petit déj.: 17 F - Menus: 60/120 F + carte -Ouvert T.A. - Restaurant: 70 couverts - Garage - Ag. - Chiens acceptés - Parking - Cartes de crédit.

• **LE RELAIS DU VIADUC** - 25, avenue de Verdun bp 7 - ☎ (33) 45.02.68 LOGIS DE FRANCE - 10 ch.: 55/125 F - Menus: 35/180 F - Petit déj. 14 F - P.: 140/180 F - 1/2 P.: 110/150 F - Restaurant: 75 + 50 couverts - Fermé 2e quinz, de fév. et du 7 au 30 sept. - Parking - Tél. ds les ch. - Chiens acceptés - Ag. - Cartes de crédit.

HOTEL LE PARVIS - Place de la Cathédralè - ☎ (33) 45.13.55 14 ch.: 80/125 F - Menus : 40/80 F + carte - Petit déj. 11,10 F - Ouvert T.A. Restaurant: 40 + 20 couverts - Tél. ds les ch. - Ag. Chiens acceptés.

* **HOTEL LE MODERNE** - 25, boulevard Alsace-Lorraine - ☎ (33) 45.13.77 17 ch.: 78/125 F - Petit déj.: 34/50 F + carte - P.: 170 F - 1/2 P.: 139,50 F - Ouvert du 15 janv. au 15 déc. - Restaurant: 40 couverts - Parking - Garage - Animaux acceptés - Change - Cartes de crédit.

HOTEL LES TROIS PILIERS - 11 et 13, rue des Halles - ☎ (33) 45.01.31 10 ch.: 70/90 F - Petit déj. : 12 F - Ouvert T.A. - Sans restaurant - Animaux acceptés.

2 You are to travel through France on the motorways with your family. You have sent for and received this leaflet. Help your parents to understand it.

1 Why is the situation of the ANRHA hotels important?

2 When booking a room, what two steps do you have to take if you intend to arrive after 7 pm at the hotel?

3 Describe a typical room at a ANRHA hotel.

4 What extra facilities do ANRHA hotels often have?

5 Why do ANRHA hotel prices vary from one hotel to the next?

Hôtels et Motels

Les hôtels de l'A.N.R.H.A. sont tout spécialement adaptés à vos voyages par autoroute, installés à proximité de ces dernières mais suffisamment à l'écart pour vous assurer du meilleur repos, ils vous offrent la possibilité d'une nuit calme et reposante sans perte de temps.

Pour réserver, il vous suffit de téléphoner directement à l'hôtel où vous souhaitez séjourner ; votre demande sera immédiatement enregistrée et vos réservations seront maintenues jusqu'à 19 heures le jour de votre arrivée. Pour une arrivée plus tardive, l'envoi d'un acompte, d'un bon d'agence de voyage, d'un écrit de société garantissant le paiement ou d'une "garantie carte de crédit" vous permettra d'arriver à n'importe quel moment de la nuit. Mais cependant, n'oubliez pas de nous signaler un retard éventuel afin de prévoir votre accueil.

La chambre des hôtels de l'A.N.R.H.A. est spacieuse et calme, totalement à l'abri des bruits de la route. Elle est équipée d'une penderie, d'un bureau, d'un téléphone direct, d'une salle de bains et généralement d'une télévision et d'un mini-bar. De plus, un lit d'appoint peut-être gracieusement fourni pour les tout petits.

Pour votre détente, nos hôtels sont souvent équipés en été d'une piscine, d'un solarium et d'aires de jeux pour vos enfants.

Nos prix varient sensiblement d'un hôtel à l'autre mais sont toujours calculés en fonction des services offerts et ce au meilleur coût.

1 It is your first day at your exchange partner's house. For your diary, write in French a short description of the different parts of the house, using these headings.

Ma chambre ....

....

Les autres pièces de la maison:
Au rez-de-chaussée ....

....

Au premier étage ....

....

Le jardin ....
La situation de la maison ....

....

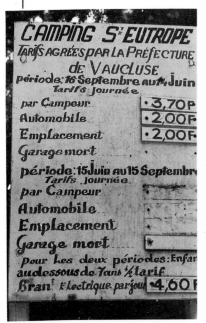

2 Your parents plan to take you and your brother or sister on holiday to Brittany next summer. They have asked you to write to the hotel of their choice to make a booking. Write a letter in French of about 80 words making the following points:

– Say that you will spend the second fortnight in August at the hotel and that you would like to make a reservation.

– Explain that you will require two double rooms, one for your parents and one for your brother or sister and yourself.

– Ask if the hotel also serves meals.

– Ask the price per person per night.

3 Write a letter in French of about 80 words to your penfriend and make the following points:

– Accept his/her invitation to go camping with his/her family.

– Ask for how long you are invited and ask the exact dates too.

– Ask when and where exactly you will be met.

– Ask if you could have more information about the campsite, the facilities and the area.

– Say you look forward to your holiday.

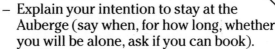

1 Write a letter in French of about 100 words to L'Auberge de Jeunesse d'Orange, Orange 84100, France. Make the following points:

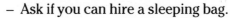

L'Auberge de Jeunesse d'Orange,
Orange 84100,
France

- Explain your intention to stay at the Auberge (say when, for how long, whether you will be alone, ask if you can book).
- Ask if you can hire a sleeping bag.
- Ask for opening and closing times.
- Enquire about rules and regulations.
- Ask for the times of meals.
- Ask about prices.

2 Write a story of about 100 words in French based on the notes below:

- arrivée de la famille Durand à l'hôtel (décrivez la famille- accueil à la réception – on leur demande s'ils ont réservé – ils sont arrivés comment? à quelle heure?)
- pris le dîner à 20 heures (qu'est-ce qu'ils ont mangé?)
- sortis en ville (où? pour quoi faire?)
- rentrés à 23 heures – demandé leur clef (à qui? quel est le numéro de la chambre? c'est à quel étage?) – montés dans leur chambre (décrivez la chambre) – se sont préparés pour le lendemain (où iront-ils?) – se sont endormis tout de suite

3 Study the pictures below and tell the story in French.

6 BASIC Listening

POST AND TELEPHONES

1 You are at a French post office. Listen carefully to the information you are given and answer the questions below. The tape is in short sections and you will hear each section twice.

Section 1

How much is a stamp to send
    a) a postcard to England?
    b) a letter to England?

Section 2

If you sent the following telegram:
ARRIVERAI SAMEDI MATIN PAR TRAIN, how much would you have to pay?

Section 3

To which telephone booth are you sent?

Section 4

You are at the counter called *Poste Restante*. What are you asked for?

Section 5

Where is the postbox in that post office?

2 ON THE PHONE

Listen carefully to the tape. It is in short sections and you will hear each section twice.

Section 1

The caller is speaking to the operator. What does she want to know?

Section 2

The service used by this caller is *Renseignements Annuaire*. What is it?

Section 3

Why did this caller ring the operator?

Section 4

Which emergency service is this caller using?

Section 5

The service used by this caller is *Horloge Parlante*. What is it?

Section 6

How do you know that this is a recording?

Section 7

Why is an ambulance requested?

Section 8

This service is often used by motorists. Why?

Section 9

What kind of information does the caller want?

3 John is at a post office in France asking about letters he has been expecting but hasn't received. He is at the counter. Listen carefully to the conversation on the tape, which you will hear twice, and then answer the questions.

1   How long has John been in France?
2   Where is he staying?
3   What reason does John suggest for not having received letters from his parents?
4   Which four personal details is John asked to provide?

1

Your exchange partner's sister, who works at the post office, is behind the counter *Renseignements/Reclamations*. Her job is to solve people's problems, answer their questions and pass on their complaints. See if you can understand what her next four customers want. Listen to the tape carefully. It is in sections and you will hear each section twice.

Section 1
What is this man's problem?

Section 2
What is this man's problem?

Section 3
What does this customer want to know?

Section 4
What is this customer complaining about?

2

You are at your partner's home. It is late evening and you and the family are listening to the radio. The tape is in sections and you will hear each section twice. Read the questions for each section before you attempt any of the answers.

Section 1
1 Who is Monsieur Béranger?
2 Why has he been invited on the programme?
3 When was the latest increase in postal charges?
4 How was the cost of a telephone call increased?

Section 2
How does Monsieur Béranger justify the latest increase in telephone charges?

Sections 3, 4, 5, 6
From the list below, choose the word/phrase that best describes the speaker's attitude:

disappointed
very happy
furious
reasonably happy
disapproving
unconcerned

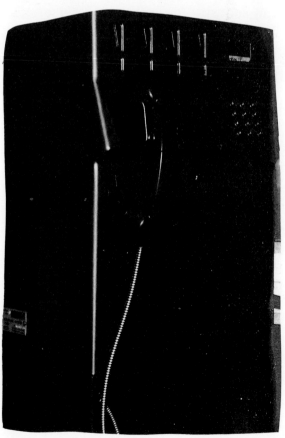

6 BASIC Speaking

Work in pairs. In each section, one person plays an English-speaking visitor in a French post office, the other plays an assistant behind the counter.

a) Pour acheter des timbres

VISITOR	ASSISTANT
Ask how much a stamp for your country costs.	State a suitable price.
Ask for two stamps.	Say how much that will be.
Give a 50 franc note and ask where you can post your letters.	Say in the box outside. Count out the change required.
Say thank you and goodbye.	

b) Pour téléphoner

VISITOR	ASSISTANT
You wish to phone home. Ask if this is the right place for telephoning overseas.	Say yes. Ask which country.
Reply and ask if you can make a reverse charge call.	Say yes. Ask the number required and the visitor's name.
Give your home number and your name.	Say which booth he/she should enter.
Thank the assistant.	

c) Pour envoyer un télégramme

VISITOR	ASSISTANT
Say you would like to send a telegram to your country.	Explain that he/she will have to fill in a form.
Ask where the forms are.	Tell him/her where the forms are (e.g. on the left/by the wall).
Ask the price per word.	State a suitable price.
Ask how long it will take to be delivered.	Give a suitable answer (e.g. a few hours, or the next morning, etc).

d) A la poste restante

VISITOR	ASSISTANT
Give your name and ask if there is anything for you.	Ask for a proof of identity.
Ask if your passport will do.	Agree, and hand over a letter.
Ask how much there is to pay.	State price (. . . francs . . . centimes).
Pay, thank the assistant, and say goodbye.	

1 Répondez aux questions.

1 Qu'est-ce que ça veut dire, P et T?

2 Dites au moins trois choses qu'on peut faire en France à la poste.

3 Pourquoi est-il plus cher d'envoyer un télégramme que d'envoyer une lettre?

4 Si vous écrivez en France, combien de temps faut-il avant que votre lettre arrive, pensez-vous?

5 Qu'est-ce qu'on peut mettre dans une boîte aux lettres?

6 Qu'est-ce que c'est, la poste restante?

7 Qu'est-ce que c'est, un jeton de téléphone?

8 A quoi ça sert, l'annuaire téléphonique?

9 Si vous téléphonez à votre correspondant(e), vous le faites pendant la journée ou le soir? Pourquoi?

10 Qu'est-ce que ça veut dire, téléphoner en PCV?

2 Work in pairs. An English-speaking pupil staying with his/her French exchange partner wants to phone Pierre, a friend of the exchange partner, to confirm arrangements previously made for tomorrow, but it is Pierre's cousin who answers the phone. One of you plays the English-speaking pupil, the other the exchange partner and Pierre's cousin.

ENGLISH-SPEAKING PUPIL	EXCHANGE PARTNER
Ask if you can use the phone.	Say yes, of course. Ask whether he/she knows what to do.
	COUSIN
Say yes. Pick up the receiver and dial 62.31.85, saying each number aloud.	Answer with a simple greeting.
Ask for confirmation of the number.	Say that's right.
Introduce yourself and ask to speak to Pierre.	Say Pierre is out and it is his cousin speaking.
Say you didn't hear what was said; ask him/her to speak louder.	(*louder*) Repeat the information and ask if that's better.
Say yes. Explain that you are ringing from your partner's and ask if Pierre can ring you later.	Say yes, of course.
Give your partner's number (22.45.94). Say you'll be out between 6 and 8 pm. Ask if Pierre can ring after 8 pm.	Say you'll pass on the message.
Thank Pierre's cousin and say goodbye.	Say goodbye.

HEURES

Sauf entre intimes, n'appelez jamais avant 9 heures du matin ni après 9 heures du soir. Attention au décalage horaire si vous ne voulez pas réveiller à 3 heures du matin vos amis à l'autre bout du monde.

1

1 At what times are you advised to use the phone?

2 When you phone someone who lives on the other side of the world, why is it advisable to think of the time difference?

Erreur

Au lieu d'avoir Martine au bout du fil, vous tombez sur une vieille dame apeurée. Ne raccrochez pas brutalement. Excusez-vous. Mais veillez à ne pas faire de mauvais numéros en pleine nuit. Vous décrochez. C'est une erreur. Faites-vous confirmer le numéro demandé (de toute façon, refusez de dire votre nom si on vous le demande). Si la personne vous présente des excuses, acceptez-les aimablement, même si vous avez été réveillée au petit matin.

Rappel

Si une conversation a été coupée, c'est celui qui a appelé qui doit rappeler, que ce soit de Paris ou de Miami.

4 If your telephone conversation has been cut off, who is supposed to call again?

Secret

Ne le confiez pas au téléphone qui a souvent plus d'une oreille sur votre ligne.

2

1 If you dial the wrong number, what are you advised to say first?

2 If someone rings you and has dialled the wrong number, what are you told to ask the caller to do?

3 How are you told to react to an apology from a caller who dialled the wrong number?

5 Why should you not tell secrets over the phone?

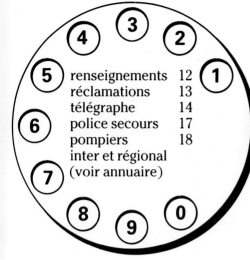

renseignements 12
réclamations 13
télégraphe 14
police secours 17
pompiers 18
inter et régional
(voir annuaire)

3

Which number should you dial to do the following?

a) send a telegram
b) call the fire brigade
c) ask for information
d) call the police
e) make a complaint

1 What is the latest time you can catch the post
  a) on a Wednesday?
  b) on a Saturday?
2 Are there collections on Sundays?
3 Should a newspaper be posted in this letterbox?

POSTES

HEURES
DES LEVÉES
JOURS OUVRABLES
11 H 45
SAMEDI
11 H 30
DIMANCHE
PAS DE LEVÉES
BUREAU
LE PLUS PROCHE

NE PAS JETER DE JOURNAUX
DANS CETTE BOITE

POUR OBTENIR 1 CARNET
DE 10 TIMBRES A 2.20 FRANCS
.Mettre 2 pièces de 10 francs et une pièce
de 5 francs. l'appareil rend 3 francs
.Tirer à fond le tiroir et se servir
.Repousser le tiroir

carnets de timbres poste

5

1 Which coins do you need to operate the machine?
2 What change does the machine give you?
3 What are you asked to do when you have your stamps?

1 Agenda

Why are you advised to keep the phone number in your address book up to date?

If you wish to speak to someone other than the person answering the phone, how should you ask?

Bureau

Why are people asked to keep their telephone calls short when phoning from work?

Cabine

When you use a telephone box, how can you show consideration to other users?

Prima

Usages

FEVRIER 1986

A à Z Le savoir-téléphoner

PTC ●

Agenda

Il faut tenir son répertoire de téléphone bien à jour. Ce n'est pas une solution de téléphoner à Paul pour avoir le numéro de Jean.

"Allô, 40.00.00.00 ?"

Il faut toujours commencer par demander confirmation du numéro. « Bonjour Madame » (que ce soit la grand-mère qui réponde ou la femme de ménage, elles ont droit elles aussi d'exister). « Emilie Baron à l'appareil » (on décline son identité). « Pourrais-je parler à Jean Dulac ? ». Mais on ne dit jamais de but en blanc : « Allô, je voudrais parler à Jean Dulac », même en ajoutant s'il vous plaît.

attendent leur tour pour téléphoner. Et si l'on a deux ou trois coups de fil à passer, ne pas hésiter à s'interrompre pour laisser un moment la place à la personne suivante.

Bureau

A déplorer : les coups de fil interminables qui bloquent les lignes (et le travail), et la série des coups de fil personnels réservés pour le bureau... parce qu'ils ne coûtent rien.

Cabine

Ne pas faire semblant d'oublier, parce qu'on a envie de parler longuement, que d'autres

Comment rester en contact durant votre séjour dans notre pays

Service téléphonique international

Appels directs

Grâce au système automatique international, vous pouvez téléphoner facilement et rapidement dans plus de 125 pays qui représentent environ 90% des postes téléphoniques en service dans le monde, et le coût de ces communications est probablement moins élevé que vous ne le pensez.

Quel numéro composer

Quel que soit le lieu où vous appeliez, vous devez composer le numéro international complet. Celui-ci se compose le plus souvent de 4 éléments distincts.

Pour appeler par exemple le numéro (28) 55 29 90 à Dunkerque, France, il faut composer:

010 Indicatif international	33 Indicatif du pays (France)	28 Indicatif régional	55 29 90 Numéro de l'abonné

N'oubliez pas qu'il faut omettre le zéro placé au début de l'indicatif régional, sauf pour appeler Andorre ou l'URSS, pays pour lesquels vous devez composer le zéro. Si vous appelez la Finlande, l'Islande ou l'Espagne, ne composez pas le 9 placé au début de l'indicatif. Certains pays ne possèdent pas d'indicatif régional pour les appels directs. Dans ce cas, composez le numéro de l'abonné immédiatement après l'indicatif du pays.

Composez attentivement le numéro sans longues poses entre les chiffres. Une minute peut être nécessaire au système automatique de connexion pour établir la communication.

Rappelez-vous que vous paierez moins cher si vous téléphonez durant les heures où le tarif allégé est en vigueur, c'est-à-dire après 20h et avant 8h, ainsi que durant les week-ends. Ce tarif s'applique à la plupart des pays.

2 Your partner's family, who live in Avignon, have a telephone number which is 81.01.60. The code is 90.

1 Tell your partner exactly what to dial to phone home from outside France.

2 How long might your partner have to wait before the call is answered?

3 Advise your partner as to the times when the phone can be used at a reduced rate.

PHILATELIE SERVICE

LA POSTE

3

1 What kind of service is the post office advertising here?

2 Explain two of the benefits of this service to its users.

3 What two steps have to be taken for you to use this service?

4 Once a member, what must you do at least once a quarter?

5 If your personal details and requirements change, what should you do?

6 How can you cancel your membership?

Pour constituer votre collection de timbres-poste, les PTT vous proposent un moyen simple et efficace :

LA RESERVATION AU BUREAU DE POSTE

Pour vous garantir la continuité de votre collection, pour vous éviter de nombreux déplacements et des pertes de temps, les PTT vous proposent de faire réserver vos timbres par le bureau de poste de votre choix.

Modalités pratiques

• Pour réserver vos timbres, il vous suffit de remplir un bulletin de réservation et de le remettre au guichet du bureau de poste de votre choix.

• Celui-ci ouvre un dossier à votre nom et vous réserve systématiquement les timbres-poste au fur et à mesure des émissions.

• Vous avez la possibilité de faire varier le nombre de timbres «réservés» selon leur catégorie (exemple : série artistique : 10 exemplaires, timbres-poste avec surtaxe : 5 exemplaires).

Dans toute la mesure du possible, votre bureau de poste pourra satisfaire également les services particuliers (découpage, bord de feuille, etc.).

• Quand vous le voulez, mais au moins une fois par trimestre, vous allez au bureau de poste retirer vos timbres réservés contre paiement de la somme correspondante.

• Si vous désirez modifier les caractéristiques de votre réservation, et en cas de changement d'adresse ou d'état civil, informez sans retard votre bureau de poste : cela vous garantira le bon fonctionnement de votre réservation.

• Si vous décidez d'y mettre fin, faites immédiatement connaître votre résiliation par simple lettre adressée au receveur de votre bureau de poste.

VOTRE TÉLÉPHONE

RÉGION PARISIENNE
Composez le numéro à 7 chiffres de votre correspondant.

PROVINCE
Province automatique : composez le 15 (pour les départements marqués d'un astérisque) ou le 16 (pour les autres départements), attendez la deuxième tonalité, composez l'indicatif téléphonique interurbain correspondant suivi du numéro à 6 chiffres de l'abonné demandé.

Province manuelle : composez le 10, attendez la deuxième tonalité, composez l'indicatif téléphonique interurbain correspondant puis indiquez à la téléphoniste le numéro, la localité de rattachement et le groupement de l'abonné demandé.

TÉLÉPHONE MOINS CHER
Les communications interurbaines obtenues en AUTOMATIQUE ou en SEMI-AUTOMATIQUE bénéficient d'une réduction de 50 % la nuit, de 20 heures à 8 heures; et toute la journée les dimanches et jours de fêtes légales.

4

1 Which one of these phone numbers is a real number in Paris?

   a) 282.23.32   b) 28.77.77   c) 129.223.47

2 To dial a number in France outside Paris, what must you do?
   a) dial 15 or 16
      wait for the tone
      dial the code for the town
      dial your number
   b) dial 15 or 16
      dial the code of the town
      wait for the tone
      dial your number

   or

   c) dial 15 or 16
      dial the code of the town
      dial your number

3 If you have to go through the operator to ring someone, what must you do?
   a) dial 10
      wait for the tone
      dial the code of the town
      ask the operator for your number
   b) dial 10
      ask the operator for your number

   or

   c) dial 10
      dial the code of the town
      ask the operator for your number

4 Telephone calls are cheaper at which times:

   a) between 8 pm and 8 am except Sundays and Bank Holidays?
   b) between 8 am and 8 pm and all day Sundays and Bank Holidays?
   c) between 8 pm and 8 am and all day Sundays and Bank Holidays?

6 BASIC Writing

1 Prepare some useful information for your exchange partner who is due to visit Britain this week. Write it in French. As there were some answers that you did not know yourself, you asked various people. You were told that to phone France, you must dial 010 33, then the regional code, and then the local number you want. Cheap rates are from 8 pm to 8 am. The post office is open between 9 am and 5 pm.

La poste: heures d'ouverture:

Où poster tes lettres?

Où acheter tes timbres?

Le prix des timbres?

Où acheter des cartes postales?

Où acheter des enveloppes?

Comment téléphoner en France?

A partir de quelle heure est-ce que les coups de téléphone sont moins chers?

---

2 Write a letter in French of about 80 words, making the following points:

– Thank your partner Philippe for his first letter, which you received a few days ago.

– Ask if your partner can be contacted by phone.
If so, ask for the code (town and country).
Ask the times when your partner is likely to be in.

– Tell your partner your phone number, the times when you can be contacted, and the times when you are not in. Say what you do at such times.

– Ask your partner to ring you when this letter arrives (if possible).

3 Your partner Michelle wishes to send an international telegram to her parents, telling them all the information below. Help her keep the number of words to a minimum (30 to 40), whilst still communicating the complete message.

Michelle wants to reassure her parents that she is very well – arrived safely and on time yesterday – was met by yourself and parents – enjoyed meeting your family – kind people – her room is very nice – last night she went out with you to a disco and enjoyed the evening very much.

1 Read this letter carefully, then write a reply in French (approximately 100 words) explaining the problems you have had with the post recently.

– Your younger brother collects stamps. He sometimes 'borrows' your letters from France for the stamps before you get them, and forgets to give you the letters.
– You moved house last month and have not had time to inform your friend of your new address.
– Your parents did not have the post redirected to the new address, so letters were delivered to the old address.
– You have a new telephone number, but your parents don't like you phoning France too often.
– Apologise for not writing sooner and accept the invitation for Easter. Suggest a day, time and place where you will have to be met. Ask your friend to confirm these details.

Roanne, le 16 mars

Chère Mary,

Ça va? Dis-donc, ça fait longtemps que tu ne m'as pas écrit? Il y a quelque chose qui ne va pas? La dernière fois que je t'ai écrit, je te demandais si tu aimerais passer une semaine à Pâques avec mes parents à faire du camping. Fais-moi savoir ta réponse, s'il te plaît.

J'espère que tu n'as pas changé d'adresse et que cette lettre t'arrivera. Dis-moi pourquoi ce long silence. N'oublie pas que j'ai le téléphone aussi, si tu n'as plus mon numéro, dis-le moi.

Ton amie française,

Jeanine

2 Study the pictures below and relate the story in French.

USEFUL SERVICES

1 The people you hear on this tape are either buying something, or asking or answering a question. The settings, written in French, should help you answer the questions below. Listen carefully. You will hear each section twice.

Au magasin de photographie

Section 1
What does this customer want to buy?
What else does he want to buy?

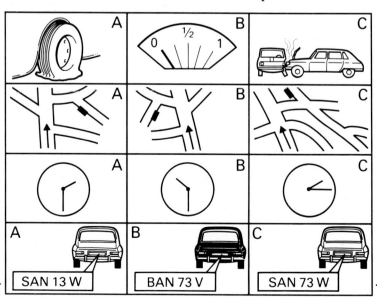

Chez votre correspondant(e)

Section 2
Which shop does this boy need?

Section 3
What is this girl asking her penfriend's mother?

Section 4
What favour is this boy asking from his penfriend's mother?

Au Pressing

Section 5
What does this customer want to know?

Chez le réparateur de vélos

Section 6
What is the problem with this boy's bike?

Section 7
What is the nature of this customer's complaint?

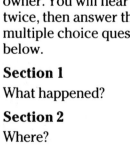

2 Listen to this conversation between a teenage girl who is speaking French on behalf of her parents, and a garage owner. You will hear the tape twice, then answer the four multiple choice questions below.

Section 1
What happened?

Section 2
Where?

Section 3
At what time is the breakdown van due on the scene?

Section 4
Describe the car.

A	B	C
(tyre)	(fuel gauge 0 ½ 1)	(car crash)
(road map)	(road map)	(road map)
(clock)	(clock)	(clock)
A — SAN 13 W	B — BAN 73 V	C — SAN 73 W

Jane and her family have just arrived in Orange by car, and have found the tourist office. Jane, the interpreter of the family, has been sent inside to ask for the information her parents want. Listen carefully to the conversation in the office. You will hear the conversation twice, then answer the questions below.

1 Jane originally went into the tourist office for two reasons. What were they?

2 Why did she have to ask the way to the town hall?

3 Where is the town hall on the map? Is it 1, 2, 3, or 4?

4 By giving Jane a plan of the town, how did the woman in the tourist office make the task easier for Jane?

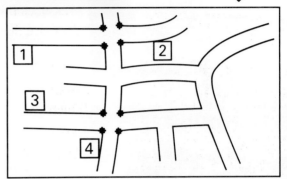

John and his penfriend Alain are at the bank. John wishes to change some travellers' cheques. Alain is waiting for him outside the bank. Listen carefully to the recording, which you will hear twice, and answer the questions below.

1 How do you know that John was queueing up at the wrong counter?

2 How did John try to avoid queueing up again?

3 How did Alain react to John's explanation of the delay?

4 What did Alain plan to do after going to the bank?

5 How many francs did John get for his travellers cheques?

6 How did the bank clerk justify the 1% commission charge to John?

You are on holiday with your family in France. Fortunately your father is a fluent French speaker. This morning, he realised that the family car needed attention. Here he is at the garage. Listen carefully to the following conversation, which you will hear twice, and answer the questions below.

1 What two problems did your father have with the car?

2 When will the car be ready for collection?

3 What was your father's reaction to the news that the car could not be repaired immediately?

4 How did your father plan to pay the bill?

5 Having made the arrangements to have the car repaired, did your father feel
a) happy?
b) angry?
c) worried?

7
B A S I C
Speaking

1

Work in pairs.

a) *Au garage*

DRIVER	ATTENDANT
Ask the attendant to fill up the tank with 4 star.	Oui, monsieur/madame.
Ask the attendant to check the pressure of your tyres.	Très bien.
Ask him/her to check the oil and the water.	C'est fait.
Ask him/her to listen to the engine.	Bon, voilà.
Ask him/her if you can have your windscreen washed.	Certainement, monsieur/madame.

b) *A la banque*

CUSTOMER	COUNTER CLERK
Ask for attention.	Monsieur?/Madame?
Say that you would like to change some money.	Bien, monsieur/madame.
Ask for the rate of exchange.	9F 20. Qu'est-ce qu'il vous faut?
Say that you want some French francs.	Bon. Vous avez une pièce d'identité?
Show your passport.	Merci. Signez là, s'il vous plaît.
Ask for a pen.	

c) *Au syndicat d'initiative*

CUSTOMER	ASSISTANT
Ask for a plan of the town.	Voilà, monsieur/madame.
Ask if the castle is worth seeing.	Ah oui, il est très beau.
Ask about its opening and closing times/days.	C'est ouvert tous les jours de 10h à 18h.
Ask if there is a special price for children.	C'est 6F pour les enfants.
Ask if the castle is far.	Non, c'est à 5 minutes.
Ask for directions from the tourist office.	Prenez la deuxième à droite et continuez dans cette rue pour 200 mètres.

2 Répondez aux questions.

1 En France, si vous voulez un plan de la ville, où allez-vous?

2 Qu'est-ce qu'il y a à voir dans votre ville? Il y a un musée? un château? un centre de sports? un club de jeunes? un cinéma? une discothèque?

3 A quelle heure ferment les magasins dans votre ville? et les banques? Vous avez un compte en banque? Si oui, comment s'appelle votre banque?

4 Est-ce qu'il y a un garage près de chez vous? Comment s'appelle-t-il? Quel est le prix de l'essence chez vous? Qu'est-ce qu'on vend à une station-service, à part de l'essence? Si vous voulez faire réparer votre vélo, où allez-vous?

Study the pictures below and relate the story in French. You may like to identify with one of the characters.

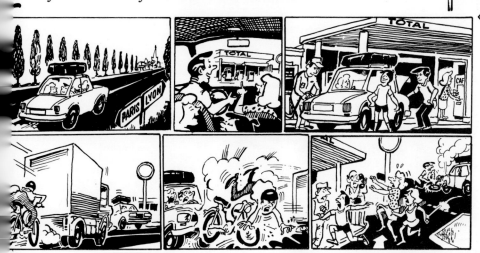

Répondez aux questions.

1 Pour changer de l'argent en France, où devez-vous aller?

2 Comment fait-on pour changer des chèques de voyage?

3 Si vous ne voulez pas porter beaucoup d'argent sur vous, qu'est-ce que vous devez faire?

4 Si votre voiture tombait en panne en pleine campagne, qu'est-ce que vous feriez?

5 En cas d'accident de la route, qu'est-ce qu'on doit faire?

6 Décrivez votre voiture (si vous en avez une).

7 Quels renseignements peut-on obtenir d'un syndicat d'initiative?

Study the picture below and answer the questions.

1 Décrivez la circulation.

2 Qu'est-ce qu'on peut acheter dans le magasin?

3 Dites ce que fait chacune des trois personnes qui sont dans le magasin.

4 Il y a combien de voitures qui doivent être réparées?

5 Comment savez-vous que ce n'est pas une station-service où on se sert soi-même?

6 Combien y a-t-il de pompistes?

7 Qu'est-ce que fait le propriétaire de la voiture à qui on sert de l'essence?

8 Qui vérifie la pression de ses pneus?

7
B A S I C
Reading

1 L'Office du Tourisme Syndicat d'Initiative

1 Is the tourist office open
   in the summer
   a) at 7 pm?
   b) at 8.30 pm?
   c) on Sundays?
   in the winter
   d) at 11 am?
   e) at 1 pm?
   f) at 8 pm?
   g) on Sundays?

L'OFFICE DU TOURISME
SYNDICAT D'INITIATIVE aux débou-
chés des autoroutes A-7 et A-9, est
placé à l'entrée du Parc Gasparin,
rénové et très agréable.

Horaires d'été : (Dimanche des Rameaux - 15 Octobre)
9 h. à 20 h. tous les jours sans interruption.
Horaires d'hiver : (16 Octobre - veille des Rameaux)
9 h. à 12 h. et 14 h. - 18 h. sauf le dimanche.
Toutes opérations de change - Réservation de chambres -
Hôtesses bilingues - Télex : 431.418 HOTELOR.
OFFICE DU TOURISME / SYNDICAT D'INITIATIVE
Av. Général-de-Gaulle. 84100 ORANGE. Tél. (90) 34.06.00
Annexe : face Théâtre Antique.

Caisse d'Epargne de
CORBEIL - ESSONNES
Place de Salvandy
C.C.P. Paris 9173-17
Succursale : **JUVISY-SUR-ORGE**
3, rue du Lieutenant-Legourd   Téléphone : 496-01-15
Mardi, mercredi, jeudi et vendredi, de 9 h 30 à 11 h 30
à 11 h 30 et de 15 h 30 à 17 heures   Samedi, de 9 h 30
                                        Fermé dimanche et lundi

2 On which two days of the
   week is the Caisse
   d'Epargne de Corbeil
   Essonnes closed?

CAISSE D'EPARGNE
ET DE PRÉVOYANCE
D'ORANGE

Siège Central   Bureau Urbain
17, rue de la République   **La Comtadine**
84100 ORANGE   84100 ORANGE
Tél. (90) 34.48.33   Tél. (90) 51.63.81

A VOTRE SERVICE
DU LUNDI MATIN AU SAMEDI MIDI

OFFICE MUNICIPAL DU TOURISME

Etablissement public à caractère industriel et commer-
cial, l'Office Municipal du Tourisme de Pau dispose
d'un ensemble de structures propres à assumer sa mis-
sion fondamentale : faire découvrir et aimer notre ville
sous tous ses aspects.

Dès lors, si vous êtes Palois d'un jour ou de toujours, un service d'accueil vous permettra d'avoir des
informations concernant :

— La ville : son histoire, ses caractéristiques, ses
   loisirs, les programmations culturelles hebdo-
   madaires etc....
— Le département, l'ensemble du territoire national.

3 Give the address of the
   branch of the Caisse
   d'Epargne et de
   Prévoyance which is in the
   town centre.

4 What is the main objective
   of the tourist office in Pau?

5 Does the information
   given by the tourist office
   concern Pau only?

Study the six advertisements for garages then answer the questions below.

1 Which two garages have spare parts for cars?

2 Which two garages could you use to hire a car?

3 Which two garages have been approved by the French equivalent of the AA?

4 Which garage would you go to to hire a bike?

5 Which garage offers special prices for students?

6 Which garage is open 7 days a week?

7 Name two garages that operate a breakdown service.

GARAGE des VACANCES
Marc DUTERTRE
Agent PEUGEOT
Ouvert tous les jours même le dimanche matin
DÉPANNAGE jusque 20 H
MÉCANIQUE GÉNÉRALE, TOLERIE toutes marques
Juillet-Aout : FORFAIT VIDANGE 150 F (4 litres)
STATION ANTAR, rue Nationale AMBLETEUSE Tél. 32.60.09

Agent

M O B I L - S E R V I C E
S A V I G N Y
L. SOLLIER
102, bd A.-Briand
91-SAVIGNY-s.-ORGE
Tél. : 921 - 46 - 15
General Motors
GM
Agréé par la
Sécurité Routière
NEUF - OCCASION
MECANIQUE, TOLERIE, PEINTURE
Dépanneur agréé sur l'Autoroute-Sud de Paris

LOCATION VOITURES - TOURISME et UTILITAIRES
LOCATION VÉLOS
11, Boulevard Edouard-Daladier
84100 **ORANGE**
Tél. (90) 34.00.34

AGENT
RENAULT
GARAGE DE LA
NOUVELLE POSTE
MECANIQUE - TOLERIE - ÉLECTRICITÉ
VENTES VOITURES NEUVES
SERVICE APRES VENTE ENTRETIEN
sur toutes ventes
véhicules neufs et occasions
" Prix spéciaux étudiants "
A 1.000 m du C.N.T.E.
30 bis, avenue Victor-Cresson
92130 ISSY-LES-MOULINEAUX
(1) 642.03.52

CITROEN PIGUET CONCESS

Piguet
LOCATION
votre concessionnaire
CITROEN
VOITURES NEUVES ET OCCASIONS
CENTRE PIECES DE RECHANGE et ACCESSOIRES
Location sans chauffeur
utilitaire et tourisme
TOUTE DUREE
★
135-137 avenue d'Italie
75013 PARIS
(1) 584.42.42

En cas de panne ou d'accident : appelez par le téléphone de sécurité. Ces appareils, implantés tous les 2 kilomètres environ, sont reliés 24 heures sur 24 aux Centres de Sécurité. Le dépanneur ou les services de secours seront immédiatement alertés.

REPARATIONS · DEPANNAGES
VENTE NEUF et OCCASION
Garage MARCHAND
S. A.
113, rte Nationale, VIRY
Tél. : 921-50-16
PIECES DETACHEES
Agent officiel CITROEN - PANHARD AUTOBIANCHI
Garage recommandé par la Sécurité Routière

8 In what circumstances should you use this telephone?

9 Explain how your problems can be solved by using this telephone.

1

1. To whom could the information given in this article be useful?

2. Before buying foreign money, what are you advised to do?

2

1. Will you be able to buy your newspaper on Tuesday?

2. Will banks that usually open on Saturdays be closed on Saturday?

3. On which day will all the department stores be closed?

4. Which museums will not open on November 1st?

5. On which day will the post office be closed?

BANQUES ET BUREAUX DE CHANGE.

Les banques sont ouvertes généralement de 9h30 à 15h30. Elles sont fermées le samedi, le dimanche et les jours fériés (certaines branches de la Barclays Bank ouvrent maintenant le samedi matin). En Ecosse et Irlande du Nord, la plupart des banques ferment à l'heure du déjeuner (pour une heure environ). Si vous avez besoin de devises pendant la fermeture des banques, vous pouvez vous adresser aux bureaux des agences de voyage (eg: Thomas Cook); aux bureaux de change dans certains grands magasins ou au comptoir de certains grands hotels; ou encore dans des Bureaux de change indépendants. Attention, ne manquez pas de vérifier d'abord le taux de change et la commission facturée (des écarts importants peuvent exister avec des commissions variant de 1% à 10% sur la somme changée).

Toussaint : ouvert ou fermé

La Toussaint 1986 un « archi-pont », qui, pour de nombreuses banques et presque toutes les administrations, va s'étendre du vendredi soir au mardi matin.

● **JOURNAUX** : parution normale samedi, lundi et mardi. Pour les abonnés, distribution assurée (sauf cas de grèves) samedi matin et lundi comme d'ordinaire.

● **BANQUES** : à Paris et dans toutes les villes où la fermeture hebdomadaire a lieu le samedi, les guichets fermeront vendredi à 16 h 30 (parfois plus tôt : se renseigner) et ne rouvriront que le mardi matin. Ailleurs (où les banques ouvrent en général le samedi) le nombre de jours de fermeture sera réduit à trois (du samedi soir au mardi matin) au lieu de quatre.

● **GRANDS MAGASINS. Samedi** : tous ouverts. **Dimanche** : fermés. **Lundi** : tous ouverts. **Mardi 1er novembre** : le B.H.V. et la Samaritaine seront ouverts l'après-midi ; les autres grands magasins seront fermés. **Mardi** : tous ouverts normalement.

● **MUSÉES NATIONAUX ET MUSÉE DES INVALIDES** : tous fermés le mardi 1er novembre. Ouverts les autres jours.

● **AUTRES MUSÉES** : le musée de l'Holographie (photographie au laser en trois dimensions) est ouvert tous les jours de 11 heures à 19 heures dimanche, et mardi de 14 heures à 19 heures (Forum des Halles). A Chantilly, le château, le musée Condé et le musée du Cheval seront ouverts mardi.

● **ALLOCATIONS FAMILIALES** : bureaux et guichets fermés lundi 31 et mardi 1er. Cependant les cliniques dentaires et les centres de diagnostics et de soins seront ouverts ces jours-là, jusqu'à 16 heures.

● **P.T.T.** : distribution du courrier normale samedi et lundi. Pas de distribution mardi. Guichets postaux fermés de samedi midi à lundi matin, puis de lundi soir à mercredi matin.

1 What is the tourist office in Hyères called?

2 How does the Mayor define the task of the tourist office?

3 This letter is an extract from the brochure on Hyères produced by the tourist office. What is to be found in that brochure?

4 Give two reasons for the pleasant weather one can enjoy at Hyères.

Le mot du Maire

Le Maire se réjouit de la toute récente promotion de notre Syndicat d'Initiative qui voit son dynamisme et son activité récompensés par sa transformation en Office du Tourisme.

Promouvoir notre ville, la faire connaître et apprécier par le maximum de personnes, aussi bien en France qu'à l'étranger : Telle est la tâche exaltante dévolue à notre Office du Tourisme.

Ce guide de la ville d'Hyères, avec ses nombreux renseignements d'ordre historique, géographique, économique, intéressera, j'en suis sûr, tous ses utilisateurs et leur fera découvrir toutes les merveilles et les attraits que renferme notre beau pays Hyérois.

Hyères offre en toutes saisons, aussi bien en hiver qu'en été, un climat privilégié que lui confèrent d'une part sa position la plus au sud de la Côte d'Azur et d'autre part, son environnement boisé qui la protège des grands vents.

Cette situation est la garantie de séjours agréables dans une ville que nous voulons toujours plus accueillante.

Je suis persuadé que ce guide rencontrera l'audience et le succès qu'il mérite auprès de nos amis visiteurs qui viendront faire connaissance avec notre belle ville d'Hyères.

Docteur J.-J. PERRON
Conseiller Régional
Maire d'Hyères

5

1 Study the home-made brochure that your penfriend has sent you about his own town.

Now make up your own brochure about your own town, in French. (If you live in a village, choose a town that you know well.)

LE GRAU DU ROI

Tourist information:	In the main street
Campsite:	Near the beach
Monuments:	St Martin's Church
	Roman ruins
Sports centre:	Out of town
Youth club:	In the secondary school
Swimming pool:	Called L'Oasis
To see in the area:	Pont du Gard
	La Camargue
Market day:	Saturday
Discos:	Le Serpent Rouge
	Le Diabolo
Cinema:	ABC - it has three rooms
Walks:	On the beach

Ville: ....

2 Write a letter in French to Office du Tourisme, 84100 Orange, making the following points:

– Explain that you intend to stay in the area for two weeks in July and that you are coming by car with your family.

– Ask what the local facilities are (hotels and campsites) and ask for price lists.

– Ask for a plan of the town and any relevant brochures.

– Ask what is worth a visit in the area.

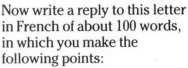

You have just received the letter below from the tourist information office in Avignon. You wrote to them on 5th June on behalf of your parents. Study the letter carefully.

OFFICE DU TOURISME
Avignon 84000

Monsieur,   le 14 juin

En réponse à votre lettre du 5 juin, je suis au regret de vous dire que pour la période du premier au 15 août, il vous sera difficile de trouver où loger. En effet, l'année dernière, tous les hôtels en ville affichaient complet pendant toute la durée du festival (du premier au 20 août).

Vous trouverez ci-jointe une liste des hôtels à Sorgues qui se trouvent à 8 kilomètres d'Avignon et qui pourront sûrement vous recevoir.

Pour ce qui concerne vos places au théâtre, je peux vous confirmer que pour les représentations des 8, 11 et 13 août, vos réservations sont faites. Veuillez être assez aimable pour nous expédier un chèque d'une valeur de 640 francs qui couvre le prix des places, des réservations et des frais d'envoi.

En espérant que votre séjour dans notre région vous sera agréable, je vous prie d'agréer, Monsieur, mes respectueuses salutations.

C M Martin   *C. M. Martin*

Now write a reply to this letter in French of about 100 words, in which you make the following points:

– Acknowledge receipt of the letter.
– Say that you are sorry to hear that it will be impossible for you to find accommodation in Avignon, and thank the tourist office for the list of hotels at Sorgues that they have sent you.
– Confirm that you want the seats at the theatre and send the cheque required.
– Ask to be sent either a receipt for your cheque or the theatre tickets themselves.
– Thank the tourist office for their help and kindness.

2 Study the series of pictures below and relate the story in French.

HOLIDAYS AND WEATHER

1 You are staying with your penfriend and his family in a French holiday camp. On your first day there, you realise that announcements are made by loudspeaker. You will hear four such announcements twice. Listen carefully and answer the questions below.

Section 1

1 To whom is the announcement addressed?
2 At what time and for what purpose are these people invited?

Section 2

3 This is an English translation of the announcement, but it contains three mistakes. Write the correct version. 'Bowls competition in teams of three players today at 5 pm. Enrol at reception. First prize: 100 francs.'

Section 3

4 On which day will the excursion announced take place?
5 Will the journey be made by car or by coach?
6 Departure time is: 8.30? 8.00? 8.15?
7 How much does a ticket cost for an adult?
8 How much does a ticket cost for a child?

Section 4

True or false?

9 Children between 6 and 14 years old are invited to participate.
10 The competitions start at 10 o'clock.
11 A darts competition is on the programme.
12 A wellington boot competition is on the programme.
13 The meeting place is the games room.

2 Your exchange partner is introducing you to her friends. As it is the end of the summer term, they are all, inevitably, talking about the coming holidays. Copy the grid into your exercise book, then listen carefully to their conversation, which you will hear twice, and fill in the information about Luc, Paul and Jeanne. Jean-Pierre's has been done for you.

	Where	When	Who with	Accommodation
Jean-Pierre	Alps	August 1-15th	Family	Hotel
Luc				
Paul				
Jeanne				

Copy the two plans below.
You will hear twice recordings of three interviews conducted
to find out French people's reasons for holidaying in the South.
Listen carefully to the first interview and complete your first
plan; then listen to the second interview and complete your
second plan; then finally listen to the third interview and
answer the questions.

Section 1 ▽

```
                INTERVIEW No 1
Reasons for holidaying in the South:
a)
b)
Activities on holiday:
a)
b)
c)
Accommodation:   in a hotel?
                 at a campsite?
                 in rented accommodation?
```

Section 2 ▽

```
                INTERVIEW No 2

Reason for holidaying in the South:

Activities on holiday: in the daytime
                       a)
                       b)
                       in the evenings

How important is the sunshine?
```

Section 3

1 What does this man dislike about the
   South in summer?
2 Why is he on holiday in the South?
3 Describe his ideal holiday.
4 What went wrong when he took his family
   on what he thought would be an ideal
   holiday?

2 You will hear a recording of the weather
forecast from French radio. It is in three
sections, and each section will be heard
twice. Study the questions before listening to
the tape.

Section 1

1 The newsreader who introduces the
   weatherman makes a connection
   between the weather and the sports
   news he has just read. What is the link?
2 What is the weather like in Brittany?
3 What will the weather be like in Paris,
   Bordeaux, and Limoges in the evening?

Section 2

4 What was the weather like before the
   rain started?
5 When and where is snow likely to fall?
6 When exactly is a significant change of
   temperature expected?

Section 3

7 Why is snow unlikely to fall today?
8 What will the weather be like in the Alps
   tomorrow morning.
9 What will the weather be like in the Alps
   and in the east of France this afternoon?
10 Write two words that summarise the
   weather of the last few days.

1 Répondez aux questions.

1 Est-ce que vous êtes allé en vacances l'été dernier?

2 Si oui, où? Combien de temps y êtes-vous resté? Vous avez fait du camping? Vous y êtes allé avec votre famille?

3 Vous êtes déjà allé en France? Si oui, dans quelle région? C'était un voyage scolaire?

4 A quelle période de l'année prenez-vous des vacances?

5 Etes-vous déjà allé à l'étranger? Si oui, préférez-vous passer vos vacances à l'étranger? Pourquoi (pas)?

6 Préférez-vous des vacances au bord de la mer ou à la montagne?

7 Qu'est-ce qu'on peut faire sur la plage? et à la montagne?

8 Est-ce que vous avez déjà fait du ski? Si oui, où êtes-vous allé? C'était quand? Quel temps faisait-il? Vous avez aimé vos vacances? Si non, aimeriez-vous ça?

9 Qu'est-ce que vous avez l'intention de faire l'été prochain?

10 Quelles vacances scolaires préférez-vous?

2 Work in pairs. One of you is a British tourist who has been on holiday in Nice, in south-east France, but travelling north to Calais today to catch the ferry. The other plays a French person whom the British tourist asks to explain this weather forecast, found in the newspaper. The route is drawn on the map. The British tourist wants to know:

1 The forecast for the south east.

2 The forecast for the north.

3 The forecast for the various other areas he/she will drive through on the way to Calais.

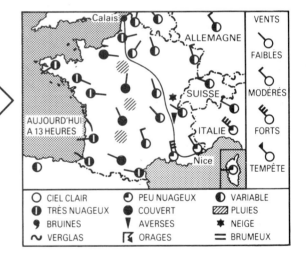

3 Work in pairs. One of you plays the tourist, the other the customs officer.

CUSTOMS OFFICER	TOURIST
Vous avez quelque chose à déclarer?	Say no, you only have your personal belongings in your suitcase.
Vous venez en France pour longtemps?	Say just for two weeks.
Pour quoi faire?	Say it is to visit your penfriend.
Vous avez votre passeport?	Say yes and show it.
Passez de bonnes vacances.	Thank the customs officer and say goodbye.

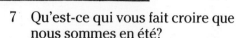

Work in pairs. Study the picture below and ask each other the questions.

1 Où est-ce que cette scène se passe?

2 Que font les enfants à gauche de l'image?

3 La dame qui est couchée, qu'est-ce qu'elle fait?

4 Qu'est-ce qu'elle porte?

5 Les gens assis sous un parasol, qu'est-ce qu'ils sont en train de faire?

6 Les garçons à droite de l'image, qu'est-ce qu'ils font?

7 Qu'est-ce qui vous fait croire que nous sommes en été?

8 Quel temps fait-il?

9 Combien de nageurs voyez-vous?

10 Comment s'appelle le sport que pratiquent les garçons à droite de l'image?

11 A votre avis, à quelle distance de la plage se trouve l'île?

Work in pairs. Last summer a British family had the most wonderful holiday in the south of France. They rented a villa found through a travel agent. This year they are keen to go to the very same place, but would like to make private arrangements with the owner of the villa. One of you plays the son/daughter of the family, who is to telephone the French owner to see if it is possible to book privately. The other plays the owner.

PUPIL	FRENCH OWNER
Say hello and introduce yourself.	Reply.
Thank the owner for the holiday you had last year.	Say you are glad they enjoyed it.
Say that your parents would like to rent the villa again this year.	Ask when.
Say that it would be for the first fortnight in August again, and ask if the villa is still available for that period.	Say that it is available.
Ask if it is possible to book without going through the travel agent.	Say yes it is.
Ask what rent the owner is intending to charge this year.	State a suitable price.

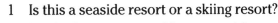

1   1   Is this a seaside resort or a skiing resort?

2   In which seasons would you consider booking a holiday there?

la joue du loup
AGNIERES·EN·DEVOLUY 1470·2500m.
LA STATION DES VACANCES D'ÉTÉ ET D'HIVER RÉUSSIES

SAINTE-MARIE

Le Village de Vacances est implanté à 500 m du village sur un terrain de 4,5 ha plat et égayé de tamaris et de nombreux bosquets.

2

1   What is the distance from the centre to the village?

2   Where can you park your car?

3   Is there a swimming pool at the centre?

4   Which of these facilities are available at the centre or in Sainte-Marie?

tennis	table tennis
windsurfing	squash
football	bowls
rugby	

SYMBOLES	
🚐	Correspondance par car
🛏	Nombre de lits
🏘	Logement dans plusieurs bâtiments
Ⓟ	Parking au Centre
🚸	Club-enfants au Centre à partir de 3 ans
♣	Institution à l'écart du village
🏓	Tennis au Centre
♿	Centre accessible aux handicapés
⌁	Piscine au Centre
≋	Distance de la plage

Loisirs: 4
courts de tennis - base nautique - planche à voile (initiation) - salle d'activités - pétanque - boules - football - hand-ball - basket-ball - tennis de table, une animation importante est organisée sur place (spectacles, découverte des traditions et de l'artisanat corses, théâtre, concerts et expositions)

EN MAISON FAMILIALE
En pension complète pour ceux qui veulent éviter tout souci de préparation des repas ou qui n'ont pas d'exigence particulière pour leur régime.

3   1   Does this centre offer

      a) bed and breakfast?

      b) half board?

      c) full board?

2   Does the centre cater for people who have to follow a particular diet?

When going on holiday, if you want to have a good time, there are precautions to take. Read carefully the advice given here, and say whether the following statements are true or false.

1 You must rest after a long journey.

2 You must take care not to exercise too intensively when it is very cold or hot.

3 To protect yourself from the effects of the sun, you must
   a) wear a hat
   b) wear sunglasses
   c) wear warm clothes

4 You must wash your hands as often as possible.

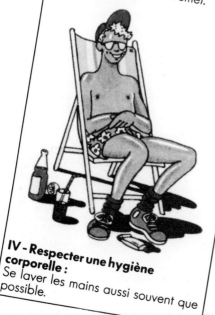

LES PRÉCAUTIONS PENDANT LE SÉJOUR

Les principales règles à respecter pendant le séjour :

I - Savoir se reposer :
Surtout après un long voyage, avec un décalage horaire et changement de climat brusque.

II - Se méfier des efforts physiques importants et prolongés :
En altitude au-dessus de 2000 m et pendant les grosses chaleurs.

III - Se protéger du soleil :
Chapeau, lunettes solaires, vêtements légers et aérés de couleur claire, produits cutanés filtrants (crème).

IV - Respecter une hygiène corporelle :
Se laver les mains aussi souvent que possible.

5 Although this centre is for people who want a self-catering holiday, it also provides a service for those who do not wish to cook for themselves. What is it?

EN VILLAGE DE BUNGALOWS
Avec logement seulement pour ceux qui préfèrent s'occuper eux-mêmes de leur restauration. Le service de plats cuisinés y sera toutefois assuré ainsi qu'un service de repas complets à la demande.

8 HIGHER Reading

A la Montagne l'Hiver . . .
This pamphlet, published by the *Ministère de l'Intérieur*, offers advice to follow for a happy skiing holiday. Read it carefully and answer the following questions.

A LA MONTAGNE L'HIVER...

Avant de partir

Renseignez-vous sur l'état des routes. Téléphonez à *Inter-Service-Routes*. Vérifiez l'état de marche des batteries de votre véhicule, des phares et des balais d'essuie-glace, le dégivrage des vitres et détenez une raclette pour nettoyer le pare-brise.

Equipez votre voiture de pneus à clous ou munissez-vous de chaînes.

N'oubliez pas d'emporter l'équipement vestimentaire adapté.

1
a) What service does *'Inter-Service-Routes'* provide?
b) List two things on your car that you are advised to check.
c) Name one item that it might be useful to take with you for the car.

2
a) When the road is slippery, what are you advised to do?
b) Find two other pieces of advice you are given in this paragraph.

Sur la route

Plus que jamais, respectez les règles du Code de la Route.

Sur chaussée glissante, roulez lentement et sans à coup. Maintenez une distance suffisante avec le véhicule qui vous précède.

Reposez-vous, surtout la nuit.

Ne conduisez pas avec des chaussures de ski.

3
a) For what reasons are you advised to get insured?
b) What signs are you asked to know and take notice of?

A la station

Assurez-vous contre les risques encourus ou que vous faites encourir.

Connaissez et respectez la signalisation des pistes et les drapeaux indiquant les dangers d'avalanche.

4 True or false?
You are told
a) not to underestimate your fitness and skiing ability.
b) not to forget to wear sunglasses.
c) always to choose a challenging skiing track.
d) that the green tracks are for beginners.
e) that there are 'give way' rules on the skiing track.

5
a) What two pieces of advice are given to people who enjoy skiing away from the proper tracks?
b) For what two reasons are you advised to take the weather forecast into account?
c) List three precautions you should take before leaving for a day skiing off the tracks.

Sur la piste

Ne surestimez pas vos capacités physiques et techniques. Entraînez-vous progressivement.

Attention au soleil, n'oubliez pas vos lunettes.

Attention à la fatigue en fin de journée.

Choisissez toujours une piste (ski, luge,...) de votre niveau :
vert : très facile,
bleu : facile,
rouge : difficile,
noir : très difficile.

Observez les règles de conduite du skieur. "Priorité" au skieur en aval. Respectez les consignes d'usages de remontées mécaniques (télé-skis, télé-sièges) et apprenez-les à vos enfants.

Hors piste et en randonnée

Pratiquez le ski hors piste c'est risqué. L'existence d'une trace n'est pas synonyme de sécurité. En tout cas ne partez jamais seul, de préférence skiez en compagnie d'une personne qualifiée.

En montagne, le temps change très vite. Tenez compte de la météo. Prenez garde, tout spécialement, aux risques d'avalanche.

Prévenez quelqu'un de votre départ, et de l'heure de votre retour. Faites connaître votre itinéraire. Munissez-vous de moyens d'alarme (lampes, sifflet, etc.). En montagne, l'hiver, la nuit tombe vite : rentrez à temps.

S'il vous paraît qu'une personne est en difficulté ou en cas d'accident, alertez les services de secours locaux.

Study the weather forecast below and answer the questions.

1. Which of these statements are true for the *Région Parisienne*?
   a) In the morning, there will be icy fog.
   b) In the morning, there will be strong winds.
   c) In the morning, the temperature will be below freezing point.
   d) Later in the day, there will be lightning.
   e) Later in the day, there will be sunny intervals.

2. Draw the outline of the map of France in your exercise book. Now read the forecast for *Ailleurs* carefully and place the symbols below on your map as accurately as you can. Write the expected maximum temperatures in various areas.

En France aujourd'hui

REGION PARISIENNE. – Fréquents brouillards, souvent givrants et assez lents à se dissiper. Ils devraient laisser la place à d'assez belles éclaircies. Vent d'est faible à modéré. La température, voisine de − 2 à − 3° le matin, atteindra 5° à 6° l'après-midi.

AILLEURS. – Sur la moitié nord, brouillard souvent givrants, avec gelées pouvant atteindre localement − 5°, (seules les régions côtières auront des températures légèrement positives au lever du jour). Dans la journée, le temps gardera un caractère brumeux, mais des éclaircies se développeront en général.

Sur la moitié sud, nuageux et brumeux le matin avec quelques gelées locales, mais des températures minimales le plus souvent positives. Encore quelques pluies résiduelles sur la Corse. Développement d'éclaircies dans la journée, mais les nuages resteront souvent nombreux près des massifs montagneux.

Températures maximales de l'ordre de 0° à 2° dans le Nord-Est et l'Est, 4° à 6° sur le reste de la moitié nord, 8° dans le Sud-Ouest, 10° à 12° dans le Sud-Est, mistral dans la vallée du Rhône surtout le matin.

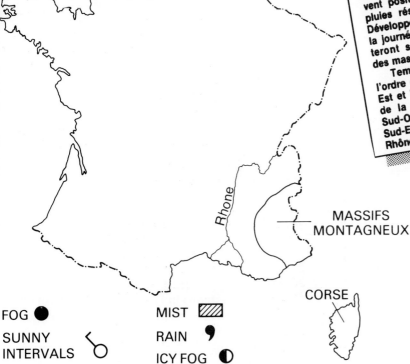

Rhone

MASSIFS MONTAGNEUX

CORSE

FOG ●

SUNNY INTERVALS

CLOUDY ◖

MIST ▨

RAIN ❜

ICY FOG ◐

8 BASIC Writing

1 Your penfriend has asked you for information about your town. Rather than sending your friend an English brochure, you decide to send your own poster written in French. Include what is worth visiting, the activities/sports in which one can get involved, the situation of the town . . .

2 You were intending to fly to Marseille today, to spend Christmas with your penfriend's family. However, it has snowed heavily overnight and the airport has been closed. You have been given a refund and have bought a train ticket immediately. Send a telegram in French to your friend informing him/her of the situation. Instead of arriving today at the airport, you will arrive at 10.45 am tomorrow at the station. Ask your friend if he/she will meet you there. Do not write more than 20 words.

MARSEILLE – MARIGNANE

CARTE POSTALE

3 You have just spent a lovely holiday staying with your penfriend, Philippe, and his family. Write a postcard in French thanking him and his parents and invite him to your home for next year. You have already asked your parents and they have said that they would be happy to welcome him. On the right-hand side write an address for Philippe.

1 Write an account in French of about 100 words of what you regard as the ideal holiday. Either describe a holiday you have already had which was 'ideal' (where it was, what you did, what the weather was like, who you met, etc . . .), or describe what you think it *would* be like.

2 Last year, you and your parents spent your holiday in the south of France. You rented a villa from M. Lacros. M. Lejean, the local estate agent, always makes the arrangements for that villa to be rented to holidaymakers in summer.

Study the letter your parents received this morning.

M. Lejean

Agence de voyages
VAR-SUR-MER

le 19 mars

Monsieur,

Monsieur Lacros vient de me faire savoir que, pour raisons familiales, il ne peut plus offrir la location arrangée pour le 10 août.

Vous pouvez, évidemment, accepter les nouvelles dates qu'il vous propose, c'est à dire du 19 juillet au 3 août. S'il ne vous est pas possible de changer les dates de vos vacances, nous avons d'autres villas du même genre, libres à l'époque de vos vacances, mais un peu plus chères. Si cela vous intéresse, faites-le moi savoir rapidement, s'il vous plaît.

Je vous prie d'agréer, Monsieur, mes salutations distinguées.

Lejean

Now help your parents by writing a letter of about 100 words in French to M. Lejean, in which you make the following points:

— You cannot take up M. Lacros's offer. You are otherwise engaged throughout July (explain how).

— You would be interested in another villa in August.

— You wish to have a sea view from the villa.

— Ask how the rent would compare with what you paid last year.

— Ask for a picture and details of a suitable alternative villa.

— Thank the estate agent for his help.

9 BASIC Listening

TRANSPORT

1

You will hear a station announcement, in short sections. Study the questions before the exercise begins and answer them as you hear each section (twice).

Section 1

For how long is the train stopping?
If your destination is Marseille, what must you do?

Section 2

Are the passengers for Nîmes asked to
a) get off the train?
b) go to platform 4?
c) travel in the front carriages of the train?

Section 3

At what time is the train due to arrive in Nice?

Section 4

Name two amenities available on Platform 1.

2

In this announcement, holidaymakers are told what to do to avoid traffic jams. Study the questions before the tape begins. The announcement is in short sections which you will hear twice. Answer the questions as you hear each section.

Section 1

At what time of the day should you avoid being on the road?

Section 2

Which roads are likely to be less crowded?

Section 3

Until which day are you advised to wait to make your journey?
During the rush hour, what should you try to avoid?

3

This is a report which advises the motorist to use the motorway (A6) whenever possible and directs him on the N7 when, for various reasons, it makes travelling easier. Study the questions before the exercise begins. The report will be heard (twice) in short sections. Answer the questions as you hear each section.

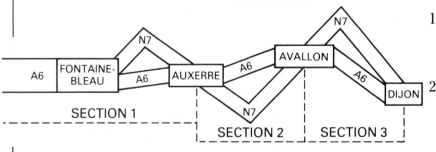

1 Copy the map and shade in the route motorists are advised to follow.

2 What are the three reasons for changing roads? (There is one reason to be found in each section.)

1 Read the questions, then listen to this announcement made on the ferry between Dover and Boulogne. You will hear the announcement twice.

1 How long does the crossing take?

2 Passengers are advised to have their passports checked
 a) in Dover?
 b) on the boat?
 c) in Boulogne?

3 Where on the ferry is the *bureau de change*?

4 Name two things that children are not allowed to do.

2 Read the questions, then listen to this announcement telling passengers at an airport that their flight is delayed. You will hear the announcement twice.

1 What is the reason for the delay of the flight?

2 How will the passengers be kept informed of any development?

3 What facilities does the airport have to serve the needs of waiting passengers?

4 What is the function of the *bureau d'accueil*?

9
B A S I C
Speaking

1 *A la gare*
Work in pairs. One of you plays the traveller and the other the ticket office clerk.

TRAVELLER	CLERK
Ask at what time there is a train to Bordeaux.	Say 8.35.
Ask if you have to change trains.	Say no, it is a through train.
Ask the price of a single ticket.	Say 65 francs.
Thank the clerk before leaving.	

TRAVELLER	CLERK
Greet the clerk and ask for a second class ticket to Paris.	Give the ticket and say its price (120F).
Pay and ask if there is a train in the evening.	Say yes, at 8.15 pm.
Ask from which platform it leaves.	Say platform number 3.
Thank the clerk and say goodbye.	

2 Répondez aux questions.

1 Vous avez déjà voyagé en train? Si oui, où êtes-vous allé? A quelle heure êtes-vous parti? A quelle heure êtes-vous arrivé? C'était direct? Vous étiez en première classe?

2 Comment venez-vous à l'école? A pied? En autobus? En voiture? Combien de temps vous faut-il pour faire le trajet?

3 Quel est votre moyen de transport préféré?

4 Décrivez la voiture de votre père ou votre mère (s'il/si elle en a une).

5 Avez-vous déjà pris l'avion? Si oui, parlez un peu de votre voyage.

6 Racontez un voyage que vous avez fait. Où êtes-vous allé? Avec qui? Comment avez-vous voyagé? Combien de temps a duré le voyage? Vous alliez en vacances/voir des amis/de la famille?

3 Study this advertisement and answer the questions in French. ▽

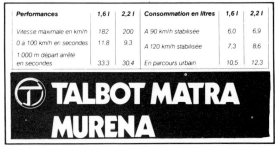

Performances	1,6 l	2,2 l	Consommation en litres	1,6 l	2,2 l
Vitesse maximale en km/h	182	200	A 90 km/h stabilisée	6.0	6.9
0 à 100 km/h en secondes	11.8	9.3	A 120 km/h stabilisée	7.3	8.6
1.000 m départ arrêté en secondes	33.3	30.4	En parcours urbain	10.5	12.3

Ⓣ TALBOT MATRA MURENA

1 Combien de modèles sont présentés dans cette annonce?

2 Est-ce que la Talbot Matra 1.6 l est une voiture rapide?

3 A quelle vitesse maximale peut-elle aller?

4 Combien de temps prend-elle pour arriver à une vitesse de 100 kms à l'heure?

5 Quelle est sa consommation d'essence: en ville? sur route? sur autoroute?

You are staying with your parents in a hotel in Lille in July. Your penfriend, who lives in Narbonne, has invited you and your family to spend a few days at his/her house. He/she phones to ask what travelling arrangements you have made. Study the information you have from a timetable and answer his/her questions.

1   Quel jour arriveras-tu?
2   A quelle heure ton train partira-t-il de Seclin-Lille?
3   Tu arriveras ici à quelle heure?
4   Où est-ce qu'il te faut changer de train?
5   Tu voyageras en première ou en deuxième?
6   Tu prendras ton dîner dans le train?
7   Tu peux réserver des couchettes à partir de Seclin-Lille?

jours de circulation
● les 3, 7, 14 et 21 juin
● du 24 juin au 13 septembre : les mardis et samedis
● le 20 septembre

horaires	n° du train	19752	9752
Boulogne-Maritime			19 30
Seclin-Lille		19 40		
Amiens			21 34
Narbonne			9 55

prestations offertes
🛏 2e
dans le train 19752
🍴 à Boulogne-Maritime
Key: 🍴 Wagon restaurant   🛏 Lit

3 Work in pairs. An English-speaking student is intending to travel by bus to see friends in Marseille. He/she telephones the bus station to find out details of the journey. One of you plays the student, the other the official at the bus station.

STUDENT

Ask the price of a return ticket to Marseille.

Ask if there are any special reductions for young people.

Ask if it is possible to leave in the morning and travel back the same evening.

Ask how long the journey takes.

Ask where the nearest pick-up point to your home is.

2 Would you be a good witness? The police are questioning you about a road accident you saw happen.

1   Quelle heure était-il?
2   Quel temps faisait-il?
3   D'où venait la voiture?
4   Dans quelle direction allait-elle?
5   Y avait-il d'autres véhicules?
6   Quel était le numéro de la voiture?
7   De quelle marque était-elle?
8   Au moment de l'accident, de quelle couleur était le feu pour la voiture?
9   Est-ce que le piéton traversait la route sur les passages cloutés?
10 Y avait-il d'autres témoins de l'accident? Décrivez-les.

OFFICIAL

State a suitable price.

Say yes and give the age group concerned.

Say yes and give departure times.

Say one and half hours.

Say that the bus station is the only pick-up point.

1
1 Is this a first or a second class ticket?
2 For what form of transport was it used?
3 Was the normal fare paid?

**Louez à Paris...
une voiture
équipée du téléphone
à partir de 155 F TTC
par jour
736.82.82**

4 What services (provided by the station) are advertised here?

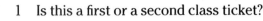

Pour les billets, les réservations et tous renseignements, adressez-vous à votre gare ou à votre agence de voyages.

5 How much does it cost to rent a car?
6 For how long can you keep the car at that price?

7 What did the person booking this ticket particularly ask for on the train?
8 How much did he pay for his ticket?
9 When and where was the booking made?

1 What sort of transport is advertised here?
2 What will you get for 395 francs?

AUTOCAR POUR LONDRES
Tous les soirs à 22 h 30 de Paris et Londres arrivée à 7 h 30 du matin. Un autocar superconfortable, pas de bagages à porter et les prix les plus bas : 295 F aller et retour. Si vous restez à Londres, une nuit dans un hôtel une étoile, breakfast compris, ajoutez 100 F. Via bus. Tél. : 354.11.99.

3 How much would you pay for a monthly season ticket?
4 Who is eligible for a free ticket?
5 If someone were to buy a weekly ticket for 22 francs, how many journeys could they make with it?

6 What, according to this, is the main advantage of a season ticket?
7 For how long is it valid?

SNCF

L'ABONNEMENT A LIBRE CIRCULATION

C'est une carte d'abonnement qui vous permet de voyager aussi souvent que vous voulez, et sans acheter de billet.
Cette possibilité vous est offerte soit sur une ou plusieurs lignes, soit dans une ou plusieurs régions. Des dispositions particulières sont prévues pour l'emprunt des TGV.
La carte est valable pendant un mois, à partir de la date de votre choix ; elle est renouvelable ensuite sans limitation de durée.

EN BUS !

TARIFICATION

1	Ticket à l'unité plein tarif	**3ᶠ10**
2	Carnet de 10 tickets tarif réduit	**22ᶠ**
3	Carte hebdomadaire de libre circulation . . .	**22ᶠ**
4	Carte mensuelle "salarié"	**70ᶠ**
5	Carte mensuelle "jeune" (− 50%)	**35ᶠ**

■ Gratuité pour les enfants de moins de 5 ans accompagnés.

8 What three advantages has Calais over other French ferry ports?

VIA CALAIS, LA TRAVERSÉE LA PLUS COURTE... 35 minutes par aéroglisseur, 75 minutes par car-ferry. Seul Calais, port le plus proche de l'Angleterre et bénéficiant des aéroglisseurs et car-ferries les plus modernes, permet une telle rapidité. A cet avantage appréciable, Calais ajoute la plus grande fréquence de traversées (de 60 à 140 par jour) pour vous faire profiter plus vite et plus longtemps de l'Angleterre. Consultez votre agent de voyage ou : TOWNSEND THORESEN, SEALINK, HOVERLLOYD, SEASPEED.

Le tunnel sous la Manche

Les Anglais : « No » au tunnel

Plus de la moitié des Britanniques — 51 % exactement — sont hostiles à la construction prochaine d'un tunnel ferroviaire trans-Manche, selon un sondage publié hier par le quotidien « Daily Telegraph ». 36 % des Britanniques seulement sont favorables au projet. C'est dans la tranche d'âge des plus de quarante-cinq ans que se trouve le plus grand nombre d'opposants irréductibles.

1 Britain is a country with strange traditions, according to this French newspaper. Name three such traditions.

2 A survey was done to find out whether or not British public supported the idea of the Channel Tunnel.
a) Give the result of that survey.
b) Which age-group had the greatest number of people against the Channel Tunnel.

Bonjour les problèmes !

BONJOUR les problèmes ! Tunnel ou pas, l'Angleterre sera toujours une île avec ses traditions si bizarres...

D'abord, ils roulent à gauche... Comment vont-ils se comporter sur le réseau français ? Et nous, en Angleterre ? Gare aux accidents...

Ensuite, le sacro-saint week-end anglais. Si nous aimons bouger et faire nos courses, en Angleterre, le « sunday closed », c'est sacré !

Enfin, les animaux familiers. Même vaccinés, chiens et chats sont interdits en Angleterre...

Les Anglais regrettent (déjà !) les ferries...

Viviers
Une dame âgée renversée par une voiture

Viviers. — Alors qu'elle traversait la R.N. 86, sur le passage pour piétons, à hauteur de la place de l'Esplanade, mardi vers 11 h 30, une dame âgée, Mme Paule Poyet née Chabert, 70 ans, demeurant « le Planjol » à Viviers, a été renversée par une voiture Renault 18 break, appartenant à la S.A. Roucaire de Vélizy, Villacoublay (Yvelines) et conduite par M. Jacques Bremond, 30 ans, ingénieur technico-commercial, domicilié à Viens (Vaucluse) qui roulait en direction de Nîmes.

Blessée sérieusement aux jambes et souffrant d'un traumatisme crânien, Mme Poyet a été transportée au centre hospitalier de Montélimar par les pompiers de Viviers après avoir reçu les premiers soins du docteur Moulin de Viviers.

Constat par la brigade de gendarmerie de cette localité.

1 Was the victim of the accident a pedestrian or a motorist?
2 How old was the victim at the time of the accident?
3 Name the driver of the Renault 18.
4 Describe Mme Poyet's injuries.
5 Who took Mme Poyet to the hospital?
6 Who gave her first aid?

3

1 You are 16 years old and wish to visit your penfriend who lives 100 kilometres away. You will be travelling alone. Which ticket will you buy?

2 Your parents and grandparents decide they want to go too. What reduction can you get?

Période bleue	Période blanche	Période rouge
en général, du samedi 12 h au dimanche 15 h, du lundi 12 h au vendredi 15 h	en général, du vendredi 15 h au samedi 12 h, du dimanche 15 h au lundi 12 h et quelques jours de fêtes.	les jours, peu nombreux, correspondant aux grands départs.

CARTE "JEUNE", 150 F en 1988, valable du 1er juin au 30 septembre : 50 % de réduction pour chaque trajet commencé en *période bleue*, et d'autres avantages (1 couchette gratuite, réduction sur d'autres services SNCF...). Cette réduction est individuelle et valable pour les jeunes de 12 à moins de 26 ans.

BILLET "SÉJOUR", 25 % de réduction pour un parcours aller et retour ou circulaire totalisant au moins 1000 km, avec possibilité d'effectuer le voyage de retour soit après un délai de 5 jours ayant comme origine le jour de départ du voyage, ce jour compris, soit après une période comprenant un dimanche ou une fraction de dimanche. Il suffit de commencer chaque trajet en *période bleue*.

BILLET "MINI-GROUPES", 25 % de réduction pour un parcours aller et retour effectué par tout groupe d'au moins 5 personnes. Il suffit de réserver au moins 48 h avant chaque voyage et de commencer chaque trajet en *période bleue*.

inconscience de certains conducteurs

LES automobilistes perdent-ils leur bon sens dès qu'ils posent une roue sur ce « no man's land » qu'est l'autoroute ? A écouter les gendarmes raconter les bonnes histoires des autoroutes, on peut le croire.

Le lieutenant-colonel Mahiou, commandant du groupement autoroutier de la légion de gendarmerie du centre à Orléans, voit défiler, en juillet, plus de 50 000 véhicules par jour. Sur le secteur de l'A 10 qu'il contrôle, entre le péage et La Folie-en-Bessin, au sud de Paris et Poitiers certains conducteurs, ou leurs passagers, rivalisent de distraction ou d'inconscience.

Bébé sur le toit

« Monsieur, le landau est mal arrimé sur votre galerie. Il bouge ! » dit le receveur du péage. « Tiens ! Le bébé vient de se réveiller ! » dit l'épouse du conducteur en descendant récupérer son rejeton sur le toit de la voiture. L'« Histoire est authentique dit le colonel Mahiou. Elle s'est produite il y a une quinzaine de jours ».

La famille est la première victime de M. Dupont, pressé d'arriver en vacances. Un père de famille, un peu trop rapide en besogne, porte plainte pour enlèvement d'enfant. En fait, Dupont junior, oublié dans une station-service, attend à la gendarmerie à 300 kilomètres de là. Quant à M. Martin, prévenant, il a installé sa belle-mère « à l'ombre » sous l'arche d'un pont enjambant l'autoroute, assise sur son rocking-chair, pour qu'elle surveille la remorque en tricotant. Et il part en voiture chercher un pneu de rechange.

Demi-tarif

A un péage, un conducteur s'étonne de la modicité du tarif : « mais c'est toujours plus cher avec une caravane ! » « Quelle caravane ? » demande l'employé. Décrochée, elle était restée 15 kilomètres en arrière. Il ne s'était rendu compte de rien.

Ces histoires qui se sont déroulées entre Pâques et fin juillet sont cocasses car elles n'ont pas provoqué d'accidents. La vitesse — le record enregistré par un radar du groupement est de 256 km/h — est souvent en cause. « Elle ne provoque peut-être pas l'accident, mais elle l'aggrave. Sur autoroute, le choc n'est jamais frontal, rarement latéral. Il faut surtout garder ses distances », souligne le colonel.

4

1 For what is lieutenant-colonel Mahiou especially responsible?

2 Write a summary of the three anecdotes related in *Bébé sur le toit*.

3 Relate in your own words the anecdote in *Demi-tarif*.

4 The colonel concludes his report with a piece of advice. What is it?

1 Study the letter Helen sent to Joëlle to thank her for the welcome she received when she spent a week at Joëlle's home.

Swindon, le quatre septembre

Chère Joëlle,

Je te remercie beaucoup de m'avoir si bien reçue. J'ai passé une excellente semaine mais le voyage n'a pas été très bon. Le train est arrivé à Calais deux heures en retard : La mer était agitée et la traversée en bâteau a duré deux heures. Arrivé à Folkestone, le train était parti. J'ai dû attendre une heure. Je suis arrivée chez moi à onze heures du soir.

Amitiés
Helen

Now write a similar letter to your penfriend, Geneviève, thanking her for her welcome. Your trip back home, however, was fine. Your train arrived in Calais on time. The channel crossing lasted 1½ hours. The weather was good. You then caught your train from Folkestone to London immediately, and arrived home at a quarter past seven.

2 While you were in Paris, you intended to keep a diary of all the interesting places you saw. In the left column, you wrote down the places you visited. In the middle column you noted what transport you used. In the right column, you wrote what you did or saw. However, as you had such a busy time, you just jotted down what struck you most on that day. You remember using a different means of transport every day. Copy the grid below and complete it by filling in the blanks.

Lundi	au stade	en vélo	C'était un bon match de foot !
Mardi			
Mercredi			
Jeudi			
Vendredi			

You were due to spend a fortnight at your penfriend's home, and be met at the station by that friend at 8.30 pm. As the French Railways have threatened a strike on the day you intend to travel, you cannot be certain that you will arrive at your destination at the time arranged. Write your friend a letter in French of approximately 100 words, stating the problem and propose an alternative in case the strike goes ahead (e.g. you might fly, then go from the airport to the town where your friend lives by coach and finally walk or take a taxi to the house).

2 The travel agent you wrote to has sent you the details you requested about excursions from Fontainebleau in August. Study his letter carefully.

Now write him another letter in French of approximately 100 words making the following points:

- Thank him for his letter.
- As you will be staying in Fontainebleau between 15th and 20th August, only book for the excursions that will take place while you are there.
- Ask him for brochures, maps and any information that you think might be useful for these excursions.

AGENCE DE VOYAGES BLANCHARD

14, RUE VICTOR HUGO
FONTAINEBLEAU

le 4 juin

Monsieur

En réponse à votre lettre du 20 avril, voici les renseignements que vous m'avez demandés concernant les excursions en août, départ de notre ville.

En car, à partir du quinze août, une journée à Paris, 150F.

Visite organisée de la Champagne, arrêt dans une cave, 200F, le dix-huit août.

Visite de notre château avec guide, 90F, à partir du cinq août, puis visite des environs en car.

J'espère que ces informations vous seront utiles.

Je vous prie d'agréer, Monsieur, l'expression de mes sentiments distingués.

Blanchard

Blanchard

ENTERTAINMENT

1 You will hear five short situations in French, twice. Read the questions before the tape starts.

Section 1
How will these people get to their destination?

Section 2
Where are these two friends likely to end up?

Section 3
Will either of these two people go to Marc's party?

Section 4
Has either of these two young people been able to get hold of a ticket for the rock concert?

Section 5
What do these two people both think of the Number One in the charts this week?

2 This recording is taken from a phone-in programme in which teenagers asked questions about their favourite pop singers or groups. Listen carefully to each call and Michel's replies. You will hear each section twice.

Section 1
Chantal
How old was Sophie Marceau at the time of the broadcast?
What is her star sign?

Section 2
Pierrette
How old was Robin Renucci at the time of the broadcast?
What is his date of birth?
How many films has he appeared in?

Section 3
Micheline
Is Ivan married?
Where does he live?
Does he have any pets?

1 You will hear twice the descriptions of four different films by a cinema critic. Listen carefully to the description of each film before writing down in a few words what each film is about, and whether the critic himself thinks they are worth watching.

2 The next passage is a recording of an interview given to Madame Nicole Gruyère, the manager of the most famous pop star ever in France, Claude François, who died at an early age. You will hear the interview twice. Study the questions before the tape starts.

Section 1

1 Give the date of Claude François' death.
2 For how long had Madame Gruyère known Claude François?
3 How did Claude François die?

Section 2

4 What engagements did Claude François have in the three days before his death?
5 When was Madame Gruyère last in contact with Claude François?
6 How did Madame Gruyère hear about Claude François' death?

Section 3

7 Madame Gruyère tells us that Claude François was full of contradictions. Illustrate this with an example.
8 Whose opinion did Claude François seek after the recording of a song?
9 Name Claude François' biggest hit, and state who was partly responsible for its success.

10 HIGHER *Listening*

10 BASIC Speaking

1 Work in pairs. One of you is buying a ticket at the cinema, the other is the employee at the cinema.

CUSTOMER

Ask what time the film starts.

Ask the price of a seat.

Buy a ticket for upstairs.

Pay and say thank you.

EMPLOYEE

Say at 9 pm.

Say it is 20 francs upstairs and 18 francs downstairs.

Give the ticket and confirm the price.

2 Work in pairs. One of you plays the French penfriend of the other. The English-speaking pupil asks the questions below in French to find out the interests of his/her penfriend.

1 Est-ce que tu aimes aller au cinéma?
2 Tu aimes visiter les monuments historiques?
3 Qu'est-ce que tu fais de ton temps libre?
4 Tu pratiques des sports?
5 Tu regardes le sport à la télé?
6 Quelles sont tes émissions préférées à la télé?

Now swap roles and do the exercise again, using some of your own questions as well as those above.

DIVISION I
(16ᵉ journée)

MONACO (2) b. *BORDEAUX (1)	2-0
*SOCHAUX (13) b. Auxerre (3)	3-0
Paris-SG (4) b. *NANCY (11)	2-1
*NANTES (5) b. Toulon (15)	1-0
Lens (8) b. ROUEN (7)	2-0
*TOULOUSE (9) b. Brest (14)	1-0
*LILLE (10) b. Rennes (20)	2-0
*LAVAL (12) b. Metz (17)	1-0
*NIMES (16) et Bastia (18)	0-0

DEMAIN A 18 HEURES
*STRASBOURG (6) - Saint-Etienne (19)

CLASSEMENT

	Pts	J.	G.	N.	P.
1. MONACO	24	16	10	4	2
2. BORDEAUX	24	16	10	4	2
3. Paris-SG	21	16	9	3	4
4. Auxerre	21	16	10	1	5
5. Nantes	21	16	9	3	4
6. Strasbourg	19	15	6	7	2
7. Lens	16	16	6	4	6
8. Lille	16	16	6	4	6
9. Toulouse	16	16	7	2	7
10. Laval	16	16	7	2	7
11. Rouen	15	16	6	3	7
12. Sochaux	15	16	5	5	6
13. Nancy	14	16	4	6	6
14. Brest	13	16	3	7	6
15. Nîmes	13	16	3	7	6
16. Toulon	12	16	4	4	8
17. Bastia	12	16	4	4	8
18. Metz	11	16	4	3	9
19. Saint-Etienne	11	15	4	3	8
20. Rennes	8	16	3	2	11

Key

Pts = *points*
J = *joué*
G = *gagné*
N = *match nul*
P = *perdu*
une équipe – a team
moins – less
avoir lieu – to take place

3 Study the football results and table carefully, then answer the questions.

1 Quelle est l'équipe en tête du championnat de football?
2 Quelle équipe est la dernière?
3 Quelles sont les deux équipes qui ont joué moins de matchs que les autres?
4 Qui a gagné le plus de matchs?
5 Combien de matchs est-ce que Rennes a perdu?
6 Quel match va avoir lieu demain?
7 Combien d'équipes ont gagné aujourd'hui?
8 Combien d'équipes ont perdu aujourd'hui?
9 Combien d'équipes ont fait match nul aujourd'hui?

1 Work in pairs. One of you is phoning the leisure centre book a table-tennis table. The other is an employee at the leisure centre.

EMPLOYEE

Allô, ici le centre de loisirs.

Certainement monsieur/madame, à partir de quelle heure?

C'est huit francs de l'heure. Combien de temps comptez-vous garder la table?

Oui, passez à la caisse à votre arrivée.

PLAYER

Say good evening and ask if it is possible to book a table-tennis table for tonight.

Answer the question and ask the price per hour.

Answer the question and ask if you must pay as soon as you get there.

Say thank you and good bye.

2 Work in pairs and take turns to ask each other the following questions.

1 Quels sont tes passe-temps préférés?

2 Tu pratiques des sports? Lesquels?

3 Combien de fois par semaine est-ce que tu t'entraines?

4 Tu fais partie d'une équipe?

5 Est-ce que tu joues d'un instrument de musique? Duquel?

6 Quel genre de musique est-ce que tu préfères?

7 Est-ce que tu vas souvent au cinéma?

8 Qu'est-ce que tu as fait samedi dernier? Et dimanche dernier?

9 Y a-t-il un théâtre près de chez toi?

10 Comment fait-on pour y aller?

3 Study the advertisement and answer the questions in French.

1 Si vous voulez assister au spectacle l'après-midi, pour quel jour de la semaine devez-vous réserver?

2 Quel jour de la semaine le théâtre est-il fermé?

3 Quel est le titre de la pièce? Qui l'a écrite?

4 Pour réserver ses places, quel numéro doit-on faire?

5 A quelle heure est le spectacle en semaine?

10 BASIC Reading

THEATRE ANTIQUE NATIONAL
CHOREGIES D'ORANGE 1988
SAMEDI 6 AOUT · 21 H 30 *
CONCERT DE DANSE
1ᵉʳᵉ SERIE COTE

RANG		PLACE
12	**PAIR**	№ **00106**

Entrée gratuite · Servitude (exonérée de l'impôt - art :134)

1 You are grateful you have been given this ticket by your penfriend's father.
a) What will you be going to see?
b) On which date and at what time will you be going?
c) How much did this ticket cost?

2

You are reading a sports magazine. To which page would you turn if you wanted to read about
a) swimming?
b) boxing?
c) cycling?

3

1 On which day of the week is the *Loto* drawn?
2 What is said about it to encourage you to take part?

4

L'auteur "d'Amour et d'Espérance"
"Sur les marches du temps"
et "Aubes nouvelles"
JACQUELINE PROVENCE
sera présente à la bibliothèque municipale
tous les après midi (sauf le dimanche)
du Lundi 25 Juin au Samedi 9 Juillet 1988

1 This writer will sign her books
a) every Sunday afternoon?
b) every morning except Sunday?
c) every afternoon except Sundays?
2 Where will she be?
3 For how many days will she be there?

5

1 With whom is this advertisement inviting you to travel?
2 By what means of transport would you reach Zagreb?
3 What is included in the price?
4 If you were expected to share, how much would you have to pay?

CINEMAS

CINEMA L'ALHAMBRA CALAIS
4 SALLES - 4 FILMS
Programme du 11 au 17 juillet 88

PINOT, SIMPLE FLIC
Salle 1
avec Gérard Jugnot.
Séances tous les jours à 15 h - 18 h - 21 h -
séance supplémentaire à 23 h 30 le samedi

BONJOUR LES VACANCES
Salle 2
Film américain.
...ou pourquoi il ne faut jamais faire confiance aux
ordinateurs, surtout pour programmer ses vacances.
Séances à 15 h - 18 h - 21 h - séance supplémentaire à 23 h 30 le samedi

L'HOMME QUI EN SAVAIT TROP
Salle 3
Le troisième Hitchoock de la saison.
Séances à 15 h - 18 h - 21 h - séance supplémen-
taire à 23 h 30 le samedi

LE FOU DU ROI
Salle 4
Avec Michel Lebb.
Un film drôle où le rire est au rendez-vous..
Séances à 15 h - 18 h - 21 h - séance supplémen-
taire à 23 h 30 le samedi

CINEMA LE DAUPHIN CALAIS
3 SALLES - 3 FILMS

LA CHASSE (CRUISING)
Salle 1
Interdit aux moins de 18 ans.
Une de nos reprise de l'été, film violent avec Al
Pacino.
Séances tous les jours à : 21 h. - samedi séance
supplémentaire à 23 h 30 - dimanche séances à :
15 h - 18 h - 21 h

ATTENTION ON VA SE FACHER
Salle 2
Avec Thérence Hill et Bud Spencer.
Séances tous les jours à : 21 h. - samedi séance
supplémentaire à 23 h 30 - dimanche séances à :
15 h - 18 h - 21 h

LADY LIBERTINE
Salle 3
Interdit aux moins de 13 ans.
Séances tous les jours à : 21 h. - samedi séance
supplémentaire à 23 h 30 - dimanche séances à :
15 h - 18 h - 21 h

A2

10.30	**Antiope**
12.00	**Midi informations météo**
12.05	**L'Académie des neuf**

Invité: Yves Dutell.

12.45	**Antenne 2 midi**
13.35	**Marianne, une étoile pour Napoléon**

Feuilleton en soixante épisodes. Huitième épi-
sode.

13.50	**Carnets de l'aventure** ℞

BIRDMAN OF KILIMANDJARO
Quatre mille neuf cents mètres de
dénivelée en deltaplane. Un vol superbe!
Réalisé par Bill Moyen avec son fils Steve.

14.25	**Dessins animés**
15.00	**Récré A 2**
17.10	**Platine 45**

Au programme : Sheena Easton « Telefone » ;
Status quo : « Ol' rag blues » ; **Christian Barham** ;
« J'te raconte pas » ; **Franck Stallone** : bande
originale du film « Staying alive », « For from over » ;
Les numéros un de la semaine et Téléphone : «
Jour contre jour ».

17.45	**Terre des bêtes**

SUR LES TRACES DE LA CHEVRE DU ROVE
Cette chèvre ne ressemble pas aux autres.
Elle est rouge, sans barbiche, mâle ou
femelle, elle porte des cornes de près d'un
mètre d'envergure.

18.30	**C'est la vie**

Architecture, L'habitat répond-il aux besoins?

18.50	**Des chiffres et des lettres**
19.15	**Actualités régionales**
19.40	**Le Théâtre de Bouvard**
20.00	**Journal**

6

1 Which cinema does not have afternoon showings during the week?

2 Why would you not be allowed to see *La Chasse*?

3 You would like to see a French film but are not in the mood for something funny. Which film would you choose?
   a) *Pinot, Simple Flic*
   b) *Bonjour les Vacances*
   c) *Le fou du roi*

7

1 If you want to know the weather forecast, at what time will you turn on the TV?

2 How many episodes are there in the serial *Marianne, une étoile pour Napoléon*? Which episode is it this week?

3 How many news programmes are there today on channel A2?

4 Your 10-year-old sister enjoys cartoons. At what time can she see some today?

5 What is the name of the programme on wildlife?

6 If you like pop music, which programme may appeal to you?

7 What sort of programme would you expect to see at 19.40?

Les Résultats de Football

Auxerre...........3
Strasbourg 0

Auxerre dut attendre une mi-temps pour concrétiser une domination territoriale longtemps contrariée par des réactions alsaciennes animées par Gemmrich et Krimau. La tâche des Bourguignons fut facilitée par une grossière mésentente entre Dropsy et Piasecki, à la 51e minute, engendrant un avantage qui reflétait jusqu'alors imparfaitement la physionomie de la rencontre, Strasbourg ayant fait mieux que de se défendre avant son naufrage défensif.
AUXERRE: Szarmach (51e), Ferreri (80e), Garande (85e).

Bastia 1
Bordeaux.........3

Les Bordelais ont enfin conquis ce titre de champion d'automne dont ils semblaient bien éloignés à la fin d'une première mi-temps où ils avaient été dominés et menés au score. Ils le doivent surtout à Dieter Muller, leur attaquant allemand enfin redevenu en forme, comme il le prouva en trois occasions devant une équipe bastiaise qui a déjà perdu huit points à domicile cette saison.
BASTIA: Zimako (22e sur penalty).
BORDEAUX: Muller (52e, 74e, 84e).

1 *Auxerre-Strasbourg* Who dominated the first half?
2 *Bastia-Bordeaux*
   a) What nationality is Muller, the Bordeaux forward?
   b) Explain what happened in the first half.

MORZINE
Haute-Savoie
16-30 ans

ACTIVITES

Stage d'initiation de 5 jours 1/2 du lundi matin au samedi 13 h : 2 h de cours par jour et plus d'une heure de tennis libre par niveau. Répartition en 2 niveaux par groupes de 4 à 5 joueurs. Raquettes et balles fournies.

En dehors de l'activité tennis, libre disposition de vélos de course, possibilité de randonnées, ping-pong, volley, trempoline, piscine, randonnée excursions...

tronomique, dansante, projections... L'entretien des chambres est à la charge des stagiaires qui participent aussi au service des repas.

DATES ET PRIX

Séjours d'une semaine, du dimanche matin pour le petit déjeuner au samedi après-déjeuner avec un repas froid fourni pour le voyage.

Chaque semaine du 01/7 au 15/9	1 460 F

HEBERGEMENT

En pension complète, à l'Auberge de Jeunesse.

L'auberge, située dans le centre ville, est une installation de caractère traditionnel.

Hébergement en chambres de 4 à 6 lits avec lavabos. Douches communes. 3 salles de réunion : bar-discothèque, bibliothèque, télé et labo-photo.

Animation prévue : soirée gas-

1 How are the students for this course grouped?
2 Apart from tennis, what other activities are on offer?
3 What facilities are available in the hostel?
4 True or false?
   a) The students have to clean their own rooms.
   b) The students have to prepare their own meals.
   c) The students are expected to help serve the meals.

This report, written by a film critic, tells the storyline of the latest film in great detail. Read it carefully and then answer the questions.

1. Give details of Christine's life before she met Rémy.

2. Who is Rémy? Give details.

3. In what ways does Christine's life change after meeting Rémy?

4. According to the critic, is it a film worth watching?

La provinciale

Film de Claude Goretta. Avec Nathalie Baye, Angela Winkler, Bruno Ganz, Patrick Chesnais...

● Christine (Nathalie Baye), une jeune Lorraine, débarque à Paris dans un studio prêté par un ami. La pièce donne sur le métro aérien. Sans travail, sans relations, Christine commence la difficile recherche d'un travail. Pourtant elle a un métier : dessinatrice en bâtiments. Cela ne suffit pas, il lui faudrait se prêter à des compromissions. La provinciale s'y refuse. Elle rencontre Rémy (Bruno Ganz), publicitaire en pharmacie, suisse, marié et père de famille. Malgré une violente passion, elle ne veut pas « être une parenthèse » dans la vie de Rémy.

Pendant un tournage de spot publicitaire pour du lait au chocolat, Christine sympathise avec Claire (Angela Winkler) qui élève seule ses deux enfants. Celle-ci entraîne la provinciale dans un milieu bourgeois. L'éducation parisienne continue.

Avec un regard tendre posé sur la dureté de la vie à Paris, pour une provinciale qui arrive, Christine restera égale à elle-même. Lucide et décidée, malgré une apparente candeur, Christine illumine ce film totalement réussi. Nathalie Baye est étonnante.

1. Quatre-vingt-dix jours à guichet fermé

Cet automne, à l'Olympia, pour la première fois depuis treize ans, les feuilles mortes se ramasseront à la pelle. A l'âge où certains font leurs adieux à la scène, Yves Montand, lui, fait sa rentrée. Certes, il sera présent, tout au long de la saison, sur les écrans. Vedette de la chanson, devenu, difficilement, une de nos rares authentiques vedettes de cinéma, l'acteur Montand sera trois fois tête d'affiche : avec Gérard Depardieu et Catherine Deneuve dans « Le choix des armes », qui vient de sortir (voir page 71) ; avec Isabelle Adjani dans « Tout feu, tout flamme », que tourne actuellement Jean-Paul Rappeneau, et dans « Le garçon », écrit spécialement pour lui par Jean-Loup Dabadie et que tournera en janvier Claude Sautet.

Mais l'événement, ce sera, pantalon et chemise marron à col ouvert, le retour d'Yves Montand sur les planches. En octobre, il retrouvera, pour quatre-vingt-dix jours, la solitude du chanteur de fond. Solitude relative : il n'y a plus une place de libre jusqu'à la dernière représentation. On a même organisé des charters depuis plusieurs pays d'Europe pour venir l'entendre. C'est que Montand est davantage qu'un phénomène du show-business. Il incarne les enthousiasmes, les ratures, les nostalgies d'une génération. Aussi ce personnage de notre temps déclenche-t-il une adhésion morale, affective, très vive du public...

Un public qui lui réservera un accueil particulièrement enthousiaste le 13 octobre.

4. Yves Montand, a French singer, is due to start a season of concerts in Paris. Read the newspaper cutting to find out more about him, then answer the questions.

1. How long is it since Yves Montand sang at the Olympia?

2. As well as being a singer, Yves Montand is also an actor. We are told that he features in three different films.
   a) Name the film that has just been released.
   b) Name the one that has not yet been filmed.
   c) Name the one that is in the process of being filmed.

3. How many performances is he scheduled to give?

4. What makes you think that the tickets for these performances sold well?

5. When is his first performance at the Olympia to be?

1 Copy and fill in the poster below, listing entertainment facilities available in your town (or those you would like to see available), e.g. la piscine.

CE QU'ON PEUT FAIRE

1

2

3

4

5

6

7

8

9

10

2 You are on a two-week exchange visit. You have been told to keep a diary of the main thing you did or where you went each day, in French. Make up your own two pages as shown here. The first entry is done for you.

LUNDI Aujourd'hui, je suis allé au centre de loisirs
MARDI
MERCREDI
JEUDI
VENDREDI
SAMEDI
DIMANCHE

LUNDI
MARDI
MERCREDI
JEUDI
VENDREDI
SAMEDI
DIMANCHE

3 Write a postcard to your penfriend explaining to him/her what you like to do in your spare time. Ask him/her if your interests and hobbies can be accommodated in his/her town too.
Useful phrases:

Est-ce qu'il est possible de . . .   is it possible to . . .
Est-ce qu'on peut. . .   can we . . .

CARTE POSTALE

1 You have recently been on a two-week exchange visit. As part of your diary, write a paragraph of about 100 words in French which relates what you did on the day you enjoyed most.

2 Write a letter in French of approximately 100 words to the tourist office of the town in France where you and your parents plan to stay while on holiday next summer. Mention the kinds of activities your family is interested in and ask what facilities for these there are in the town (cinema, sports centre, etc). Also ask for information leaflets which would include the charges and opening times of various places of interest.

3 Write an essay in French of about 130 words relating to the pictures below.

MEETING PEOPLE

1 You have just arrived at your exchange partner's home. You are told where everything is and what the rules of the house are. Listen carefully to the tape, which will be played in short sections. You will hear each section twice. Then answer the questions.

Section 1

Where is the bathroom?

Section 2

Where are the toilets?

Section 3

At what times are lunch and evening meal served?

Section 4

What is your friend's mother asking you?

Section 5

By what time are you expected to be in at night?

Section 6

By what time are you asked to be in bed?

Section 7

What are you asked to do by 8.15?

Section 8

Are you allowed to use the family phone to telephone home?

Section 9

What two chores are you asked to do?

Section 10

Where are you asked to put your dirty clothes?

2 Michael, who is staying in France, has answered the phone because no one else is at home. It is Luc, a friend of his exchange partner Pierre. He is inviting them both to a party. Copy the form into your exercise book and from the recording complete it with the details Michael needs to pass on the message to Pierre. You will hear the telephone conversation twice.

La Boum

Day . . . .

Time . . . .

Where . . . .

Who will be there . . . .

. . . .

3 Alan's exchange partner, Michel, is introducing him to his friends. Listen to their conversation carefully. You will hear it twice, then answer the questions.

1 How many friends does Alan meet?

2 How long will the exchange visit last?

3 It is not Alan's first exchange visit. When was he involved in an exchange before?

4 What was the name of Alan's partner at that time?

5 Where does the group of friends decide to go?

Peter and Alain, two exchange partners, are discussing the meal they have just had at Alain's home – at least, that is the first thing they discuss! Their conversation then focusses on comparing home life in Britain and in France. Listen carefully to their conversation. The tape will be played in two sections and you will hear each section twice. Then answer the questions below.

Section 1

1 What was on the menu tonight?
2 Did Peter enjoy his dinner?
3 How does Alain explain the difference between English and French food?
4 State two other differences between a French and an English home discussed in this section.

Section 2

5 What is Section 2 about?
6 Why is mealtime an important time for a French family?
7 Would Peter be happy living in a French family? Give his reasons.

Serge always seems to have the answer to teenage problems! Once a week teenagers can participate in a phone-in programme on the radio that Serge runs, asking for his advice and possible solutions to their personal problems. The tape will be played in sections, and you will hear each section twice. Listen carefully and then answer the questions.

Section 1

1 What is the nature of Géraldine's problem?
2 What advice is she given?

Section 2

3 What is Hervé's problem?
4 What advice is he given?

11
BASIC
Speaking

1 Work in pairs. One of you is an English-speaking student arriving at his/her exchange partner's home for the first time; the other plays the partner's mother/father.

STUDENT	PARENT
Say hello and introduce yourself in a few words.	Ask if he/she had a pleasant journey.
Say yes, you've had a good journey.	Ask if he/she has any brothers or sisters.
Talk a little about your family (who they are, how old they are, what they do).	Ask if he/she wants to rest.
Say yes, you are feeling tired.	
Present a gift to the family.	Say thank you.
Ask where your room is.	Say you will show him/her to the room.

(Un peu plus tard . . .)

Ask where you can put your clothes and luggage.	Say that he/she can use the wardrobe in the bedroom.
Ask where the toilet is.	Say it is opposite his/her room.
Ask about the times of meals.	State suitable times.
Ask what time you are expected to be in at night.	Say about 10 pm.

2 Répondez aux questions.

1 Quand avez-vous du temps de libre pour rencontrer vos amis?
2 Où rencontrez-vous vos amis?
3 Qu'est-ce que vous faites avec vos amis?
4 Combien de fois par semaine sortez-vous?
5 Est-ce que vous avez la permission de sortir le soir?
6 Avez-vous déjà participé à un échange? Si oui, comment s'appelait votre partenaire? Dans quelle ville habitait-il/elle? Décrivez votre partenaire.

3 An English-speaking student is on the phone to his/her exchange partner. They are to meet for the first time at the station the next day, and the English student is giving a description of himself/ herself to the French student.

ENGLISH SPEAKING STUDENT	FRENCH STUDENT
Give your height and weight.	Ask him/her to describe his/ her hair.
Describe your hair (colour, length, curly or straight, etc)	Ask him/her the colour of his/ her eyes.
Describe your eyes.	Ask your partner what he/she will be wearing.
Say what you will be wearing tomorrow.	

Study the picture below and then answer the questions.

1 A votre avis, est-ce que cette scène se passe dans une maison française ou anglaise? Justifiez votre réponse.

2 Décrivez la pièce dans laquelle se passe cette scène.

3 Quelle heure est-il?

4 Est-ce que c'est le matin ou le soir? Justifiez votre réponse.

5 Combien d'enfants y a-t-il dans cette famille, pensez-vous?

6 Qu'est-ce qu'il y a à la télé?

7 Qu'est-ce qu'il y a sur la table?

8 Qu'est-ce que le garçon anglais a comme bagages?

9 Comment savez-vous qu'il a voyagé par avion?

Study the pictures below and relate the story in French.

11 BASIC Reading

1

Study these small ads. Who would you write to if you were looking for a penfriend
a) in the north of France?
b) keen on sports and going to discos?
c) who likes a good laugh?
d) with a sense of adventure?
e) who collects stickers?

COPAINS COPINES

J'ai 15 ans et cherche amis fille ou garçon j'aime Elvis U2 Renaud, rire, l'amitié et la vie. **Isabelle Chalmin 35 rue Auvernon 06600 Antibes**

Fille 15 ans recherche garçon de 16 18 ans aimant le sport, Hallyday et aller en boîte. Réponse assurée **Sandrine Martin 6 rue d'Artois 51350 Cormontreuil**

Salut garçon cherche correspondant tous âge aimant la motos et aventures photo facultative réponse assurée **Philippe Sauvage Hôtel de Bretagne 72140 Sillé le Guillaume**

Je recherche des timbres, cartes postales, autocollants, souhaite trouver correspondant amical. **Laurent Raymond, 2 Rue de Verdun, 58400 La Charité sur Loire.**

Deux filles 15 ans désire lier amitié avec garçons 15 16 ans aimant le funky, cinéma et moto **Sandrine Quarcy Jean Bedel 82370 Labastide Saint Pierre**

Isabelle 13 ans désire correpsondre avec des garçons et des filles de 13 16 ans aimant Goldman, Lhermitte, Bruel, ciné, sorties, etc. Habitant le Nord joindre photo réponse assurée **Isabelle Cartron 242 rue du Faubourg de Roubaix 59800 Lille**

2

Read the following letter, then answer the questions.

1 Which class is Isabelle in?
2 How did Isabelle come to have Tracy's address?
3 Isabelle hopes to go to England
  a) for how long?
  b) at what time of year?
4 Write three things that Isabelle would like Tracy to put in her next letter.

Montluçon, le 8 mars

Chère Tracy,

Je m'appelle Isabelle, j'ai 15 ans et je suis en troisième. Mon prof. d'anglais m'a donné ton adresse quand je lui ai demandé s'il connaissait quelqu'un qui serait intéressé par un échange privé.

Voilà ce que je te propose : Comme j'ai un examen à la fin de l'année scolaire, ce serait bien si je pouvais venir chez toi, disons 2 semaines, avant juin. En fait, le mieux serait peut-être les vacances de Pâques. Qu'est-ce que tu en penses ? Est-ce que tu as des projets pour Pâques ? Pour ta visite en France, c'est quand tu voudras. Mes parents sont prêts à te recevoir.

Réponds-moi vite et dis-moi si tu es d'accord. Parle-moi un peu de ta famille. Tu as des frères et des soeurs ? Aussi de ton école. En quelle classe es-tu ? Envoie une photo, s'il te plaît. Je joins la mienne à cette lettre. A bientôt de te lire. Donne-moi de bonnes nouvelles !

Amitiés,
Isabelle

1 What is the whole article about?

2 One of the purposes of the *Aumônerie* is discussed in this paragraph. Which one?

3 List four other reasons why young people might want to go to the *Aumônerie*.

aumônerie enseignement public

Voici quelques éléments des réponses faites à un sondage réalisé en Avril auprès des jeunes des collèges et lycées qui fréquentent l'AEP (Aumônerie de l'Enseignement Public)

ETRE ENSEMBLE (j'adore ça)

Les mots "être ensemble", "se regrouper", "se réunir", "se rencontrer" reviennent souvent. C'est "pour le plaisir des jeunes, qu'on vient", "ça apprend à s'exprimer", on est "libérés, débarrassés" des parents. Contre l'ennui, la solitude. Pour l'ambiance. Sans l'aumônerie je ne connaitrais pas de jeunes. Certains "qui ne se connaissaient pas au début, sont devenus amis", d'autres remarquent "je ne suis plus venu car j'ai été mal accueilli" et demandent "plus de gentillesse les uns envers les autres".

"C'est le seul endroit où on peut rencontrer d'autres jeunes", "on peut se réunir autre part qu'au lycée".

SERIEUX S'ABSTENIR!

L'enquête fait remarquer une coexistence pacifique entre plusieurs types d'expressions: "Entre la semaine de travail et le boulot qui nous attend le week-end, l'AEP ça détend" "On rigole", "on foire" on fait des bêtises"
ET
"Il manque une salle de prière", "on veut du sérieux", "du calme", on déplore un manque d'organisation voire d'obligation dans l'animation des groupes, d'autres au contraire apprécient "l'auto-discipline".

LE DROIT A LA PAROLE

Le ton de cette série de réponse est net, on sent une nécessité viscérale de discuter chez les jeunes.

"A l'AEP on peut discuter de ce qu'on veut, entre jeunes de notre âge, avec des plus âgés". Bavarder, bien s'entendre, débattre, sont des expressions qui reviennent le plus souvent. "L'AEP est lieu qualifié" pour discuter de choses intéressantes de faits marquants de la semaine, de la vie quotidienne, scolaire on parle de religion.

4 Another purpose of the *Aumônerie* is presented in this paragraph. Which one?

5 Name three of the topics often discussed at the *Aumônerie*.

6 In the first part of this paragraph, we are told that some young people like to go to the *Aumônerie*. Explain their reasons for doing so.

7 Is the tone of the second part of this paragraph
a) supportive?
b) critical?
c) angry?

11 BASIC Writing

1

Study the small ads below carefully. Then write a similar *petite annonce* in which
a) you introduce yourself
b) you explain what kind of person you would like to write to.

COPAINS COPINES

J'ai 15 ans et je désire correspondre avec garçons et filles très sympas de 14 17 ans réponse assurée **Angéla Pader 11 rue de la Tuilerie 55800 Revigny-sur-Ornain**

Jeune fille 15 ans désire correspondre avec jeune homme ayant 15 18 ans aimant le cheval, le disco et écrire espère amitié **Nathalie Bellanger 12 Avenue De Charlebourg 92250 La Garenne Colombes**

2

You have just returned from Orange, where for the last two weeks your exchange partner's family have really made you feel welcome in their home. Write them a postcard in French of 30–40 words, thanking them for their hospitality and inviting Annie, your partner, to stay in your home when the French party visits England.

CARTE POSTALE

Mlle Annie Mouthuisson
3, rue Victor Hugo
84100 ORANGE
FRANCE

3

Write a letter in French of about 80 words in which you reply to this advertisement:

- Introduce yourself and your family.
- Say you have wanted to have a French penfriend for a long time.
- List your hobbies.
- Say what you think of Martine's hobbies.
- Say that you wish to write in French, and have your mistakes corrected.
- Enclose a photo. Don't forget to give Martine your address.

Jeune fille 16 ans voudrait correspondre avec anglais(e) aimant musique photo ciné sorties et sports joindre photo merci. **Martine Boussin 6, rue de Guise, ORANGE, 84100**

1 Study these three documents carefully.

CAUSE GREVE DES TRAINS, ECHANGE REPORTE D'UN JOUR

CHAQUE PARTICIPANT DOIT CONFIRMER PAR L'INTERMEDIAIRE DE SON

PARTENAIRE QUE CA NE PRESENTE PAS DE PROBLEMES

JEAN-MARIE CHABOT (ORGANISATEUR FRANCAIS)

Programme de l'echange (1ère semaine)

Mardi 12: Arrivée à la gare Saint-Martin des Anglais 20 heures 15. Les familles viennent chercher le partenaire anglais de leur enfant.

Mercredi 13: Matin Réception à la Mairie

Jeudi 14: Après-midi Visite du lycée

Vendredi 15: Excursion en car (pique-nique sur la plage)

Matin Visite de l'usine de chocolat

Après-midi Hypermarché

Samedi 16 et Dimanche 17: En famille

Now write a letter in French of about 100 words to your partner Pierre making the following points:

- You have read the programme of the exchange and the telegram sent by the French leader.
- Confirm what the French organiser is asking you to confirm in the telegram.
- Answer Pierre's question, i.e. suggest arrangements for meeting him, transport from pick-up point, time of arrival at his home.
- Ask how the rest of the programme will be affected and suggest a suitable alteration.

Lorient, le 4 juin

Chère Sandra,

Tu sais sûrement que la date de l'échange à été changée. Comme mon père doit assister à une conférence le mercredi 13, il nous sera impossible de venir te chercher en voiture à la gare ce jour-là. Comment penses-tu qu'on devrait s'organiser pour se rencontrer?

Pierre

2 When staying in France with your exchange partner, you attended a fancy-dress party and met many young French people. Write a short account of the event for your partner's school magazine, describing who you met and what their disguise was.

HEALTH

12 BASIC Listening

1 You will hear ten short passages recorded in a doctor's surgery. Some are questions the doctor might ask you, some deal with what he might ask you to do while he examines you, and others are his instructions after examination. Listen to the tape carefully, which is in short sections. You will hear each section twice, then answer the question.

Section 1

What is the doctor asking you?

Section 2

How many tablets a day are you told to take?

Section 3

What are you told to do?

Section 4

When does the doctor want to see you again?

Section 5

What two things are you not allowed?

Section 6

What are you told to do for two hours every afternoon?

Section 7

Where is the patient told to go straightaway?

Section 8

What is the doctor telling you to do?

Section 9

What is the doctor asking you?

Section 10

According to the doctor, are you suffering from anything serious?

2 Your penfriend attends a first aid class, and has invited you to accompany him. Listen carefully to the teacher, who today deals with the ailments listed below. Match the treatments with the complaints (number with letter). You will hear the tape twice.

Useful vocabulary:
une brûlure – a burn
une coupure – a cut

DOCTEUR ANNICK VERHÉE-PULVÉRY

MEDECINE GENERALE

3 Peter, an English boy on an exchange visit, did not quite understand what the French doctor told him, so he took his prescription to the chemist with the intention of asking him to repeat what the doctor had said. Listen carefully to their conversation. You will hear the tape twice, then answer the questions below.

Ailments

1   A burn
2   A minor cut
3   A slightly more serious cut
4   An insect bite
5   A broken limb

Treatments

A   Call an ambulance
B   Apply some cream
C   Put your hand in cold water
D   Raise your hand above your head for 5 minutes
E   Press hard on it

1   Copy and fill in the grid.

2   What amount of medicine is Peter told to take when he starts feeling better?

3   How much does he have to pay for his medicine?

	How many times a day?	In what quantity?	At what times of the day?
Sirop Toussard			
Comprimés Grippalon			

1 Your exchange partner's mother wants to participate in a phone-in programme on local radio. The whole family, including yourself, decides to listen to the programme. Listen carefully before you answer the questions. The tape is in short sections, and you will hear each section twice.

Section 1

1 What is the first caller's problem?

2 What is the doctor's opinion of a vegetarian diet?

Section 2

3 What is the ailment the second caller wishes to discuss?

4 The doctor gives two useful pieces of advice. What are they?

Section 3

5 Why did the doctor think that this caller's question was a good one?

6 The doctor gives examples of minor ailments. Write down the letters of the ones you hear.

A toothache   H burn
B cut   I spots
C cold   J sprained ankle
D mild flu   K graze
E indigestion   L migraine
F headache   M insect bite
G diarrhoea

7 Why is a chemist better placed than a doctor to help with minor ailments?

2 Michael is unwell, and it is very late at night. His partner's mother has rung the doctor on call for advice. Listen to what Michael heard (i.e. one half of the telephone conversation) and answer the questions. You will hear the call twice.

1 What was wrong with Michael
   a) last evening?
   b) now?

2 List four things that the mother is told to do to relieve Michael.

3 According to the doctor, what are the likely causes of Michael's illness?

12
BASIC
Speaking

1 a) Work in pairs. One of you plays the chemist and the other the customer.

CUSTOMER	CHEMIST
Tell the chemist you have burnt your hand.	Ask if you can examine the burn.
Ask if the chemist can prescribe something for it.	Say yes, and suggest suitable medicine. Say how much that will be.
Pay for the medicine.	Thank the customer.
Ask whether you should see a doctor.	Say no, that's not necessary, it's not a serious burn.

b) One of you plays the chemist, the other the customer, who is acting as interpreter for a friend whose spoken French is not very good.

CUSTOMER	CHEMIST
Say hello and explain that your friend's French is not very good.	Say hello and ask how you can help.
Explain that your friend is suffering from sunburn and as a result has a high temperature.	Ask how long he stayed out in the sun.
Say that he stayed out in the sun all yesterday afternoon.	Ask him to take his shirt off.
Ask the chemist's advice about what your friend should do.	Tell him to rest and avoid the sun for the next few days.

c) One of you plays the doctor, the other the patient.

PATIENT	DOCTOR
Explain to the doctor that you have a bad back.	Ask how long he/she has been in pain.
Tell the doctor how long.	Ask if there is a particular reason for this back pain.
Explain that you hurt your back while you were playing football/hockey.	Examine his/her back and say that it is not a serious injury.
Ask whether another visit will be necessary.	Say no. State a suitable price for your services.
Say thank you, pay and ask for a receipt.	Give him/her a receipt.
Say thank you and goodbye.	Say goodbye.

Répondez aux questions.

1 Vous allez bien aujourd'hui?

2 Si vous avez mal aux dents, où allez-vous?

3 Quel médicament prenez-vous pour le mal à la tête?

4 Qui peut vous donner une ordonnance?

5 Où devez-vous porter cette ordonnance?

6 Qu'est-ce qu'on peut acheter à la pharmacie?

7 Manquez-vous souvent l'école parce que vous êtes malade?

8 Combien de fois par an avez-vous un rhume?

9 Etes-vous déjà resté à l'hôpital? Si oui, combien de temps?

10 Avez-vous déjà appelé une ambulance? Si oui, pour quelle raison?

11 Combien de fois êtes-vous allé chez le docteur ce mois-ci?

12 Quand êtes-vous allé chez le dentiste pour la dernière fois?

12
HIGHER
Speaking

1 a) Work in pairs. One of you plays an English student staying with his/her penfriend's family. The other plays the penfriend's mother.

MOTHER	STUDENT
Ask your guest why he/she is not up yet.	Say that you don't feel very well (you think you are running a temperature).
Ask if your guest would like to see a doctor.	Say yes, but you would prefer to have the doctor come and see you. Ask if that is possible.
Say yes. Advise him/her to take some aspirin in the meantime.	Decline the offer and say you would rather wait and see what the doctor prescribes.

b) Now one of you plays the student, the other the doctor.

DOCTOR	STUDENT
Ask what the matter is.	Greet the doctor and explain what you think is wrong with you.
Ask if your patient is under any medical treatment.	Say no, you are not under any medical treatment.
Ask if he/she is properly insured.	Explain that you are on a school exchange and that the teacher in charge will have the relevant details. Tell the doctor how to contact the teacher.
Tell your patient he/she has flu and must rest for the next few days.	Ask if your friends can visit you.
Say yes.	Thank the doctor and say goodbye.

2 Study the picture below and relate the story in French. If you
like, tell the story from the point of view of one of the
characters.

12
B A S I C
Reading

1
1 What would you do if you needed a chemist at 10 o'clock in the evening?

2 If you needed an ambulance, which telephone number would you ring?

Bloc-notes

DE GARDE
Pharmacie. — Pons, rue des Halles, tél. 90.63.00.69.
A partir de 21 heures. — S'adresser au commissariat, tél. 90.63.01.34.
S.N.C.F. — Tél. 90.63.02.60; informations, tél. 90.82.50.50.

URGENCES
Ambulance secours. — Tél. 18 ou 90.63.15.10.
Hôpital. — Tél. 90.63.10.72.
Maternité. — Tél. 90.63.02.26.

A VOTRE SERVICE

2
1 For how long is the treatment prescribed by Dr Blanc to be followed?

2 At which times of the day is the medication to be taken?

ORDONNANCE

Mlle Smith M.   le 28 juin

Sirop Toussard
    à prendre 3 fois par
jour après les repas pendant
une semaine

Dr Blanc (Médecine générale)

3
1 What is the purpose of the *Centre Départemental de Transfusion Sanguine?*

2 How many times a year are men invited to come to the Centre?

IMPORTANT

faites **don** de votre **sang**

Si vous avez donné votr[e] sang depuis moins de 2 moi[s] veuillez ne pas tenir compte d[e] cette invitation mais demandez [à] vos parents et amis de suivre votr[e] généreux exemple.

Une femme peut donne[r] 3 fois par an, un homme 5 fois

Il n'est pas nécessaire d'être à jeun.

MERCI DE VOTRE VISITE.

CENTRE DÉPARTEMENTAL DE TRANSFUSION SANGUINE DU VAL - DE - MARNE
1, VOIE FÉLIX-ÉBOUÉ   ECHAT 629 - 94021 CRÉTEIL CEDEX

MNEF - Mutuelle Nationale des Etudiants de France
16, avenue Raspail - 94250 Gentilly

Centre 601 de Sécurité Sociale
37, boulevard Saint-Michel 75005 Paris,
10, rue Ponscarme, 75013 Paris

MNEF

Accueil
Renseignements
de 9 h à 17 h, sauf le samedi
37, boulevard Saint-Michel
75005 Paris
10, rue Ponscarme
75013 Paris

Correspondance
Accueil
16, avenue Raspail
94250 Gentilly
Tél. 664.18.18

avec votre Section locale, vous bénéficiez
de la gratuité des soins
(Aucune avance d'argent)
Pour les adhérents MNEF affiliés à la Sécurité Sociale dans de nombreux centres, hôpitaux ou dispensaires (selon les tarifs conventionnels de la Sécurité Sociale)

Centre de Santé de la MNEF
sur rendez-vous, au
22, boulevard Saint-Michel - 75006 Paris
Tél. 354.09.52

MEDECINE GENERALE
de 9 h à 12 h et de 14 h à 17 h (sauf samedi)

SOINS INFIRMIERS
Tous les après-midi du mardi au vendredi de 14 h 30 à 18 h 30, sans rendez-vous

STOMATOLOGIE ET SOINS DENTAIRES
Tous les jours de 8 h à 12 h et de 13 h 30 à 18 h, le samedi de 9 h à 12 h et de 14 h à 17 h

ANALYSES MEDICALES
Deux laboratoires, tous les matins (sauf jeudi)

4
1 Who can benefit from the services of MNEF?

2 Do the MNEF offices open on Saturdays?

3 Give the address of the MNEF health centre.

4 Name two ways in which MNEF serves its members.

INSOLATION

L'insolation ou coup de soleil peut se produire même par temps couvert ; elle se manifeste par mal de tête, nausées, parfois perte de connaissance. Installer le malade dans un endroit **frais,** en position demi-assise, tête surélevée s'il présente une face rouge, en position allongée, tête basse si sa face est pâle. Compresses froides sur la tête et appeler le médecin.

1
1 What is the complaint dealt with in this passage?
2 What are the symptoms?
3 How should you deal with a sufferer if they look pale?

2
1 Are you more or less likely to experience travel sickness
  a) if you have not had anything to eat?
  b) if you smoke?
  c) if the driver is driving the vehicle smoothly?
2 How should you deal with the sufferer?
3 Name the precautions you should take before allowing the sufferer back into the vehicle.

MAL DES TRANSPORTS
(CINETOSE)

Causé par un trouble de l'oreille interne, le mal des transports est favorisé par une disposition naturelle à l'appréhension, les bons repas, l'alcool, le tabac, le manque d'aération du véhicule, une conduite brutale ou capricieuse, des accélérations ou décélérations brusques, des conversations, des odeurs ou des spectacles écœurants.

Sortir le malade du véhicule, le réchauffer s'il a froid (vêtements, couverture) ; lui faire boire une **infusion chaude, à l'exception de thé ou de café ; pas d'alcool,** même de menthe.

Aérer le véhicule, vider le cendrier, asseoir le malade rétabli à l'avant, et repartir en évitant tout ce qui est signalé plus haut. Laisser au moins une glace ouverte. Stopper en cas de récidive.

Préventivement, en dehors des précautions déjà signalées, demander à son médecin de prescrire un médicament approprié.

3 Why are dentists worried about their future?

4 Is morale in the nursing profession low or high? Explain why.

Dentistes : le prix de la qualité

Parmi les trente mille chirurgiens-dentistes répertoriés, vingt-six mille libéraux s'inquiètent pour leur avenir. Une crainte : les centres de santé, qui donnent des soins gratuits. Les soins chez le dentiste libéral sont remboursés à 75 %. La clientèle de ces cabinets fuira-t-elle ? « Ce serait choisir la sécurité dans la médiocrité », disent les chirurgiens-dentistes.

▶ **Infirmières.** Elles sont deux cent quatre mille, dont vingt mille en secteur libéral. Avant, elles ne travaillaient que cinq ans, puis s'arrêtaient. Maintenant, certaines tiennent quinze ans. Le marché est saturé, et la profession se dévalorise. Beaucoup d'infirmières, faute de places, sont employées comme aides soignantes. Depuis deux ans, certaines quittent l'hôpital public pour tenter l'aventure de l'indépendance en cabinet libéral. Désillusion ! La concurrence, les frais professionnels étouffent l'enthousiasme. Griefs des « libérales » : une heure de soins ne rapporte que 61 F 80 ; les déplacements sont payés à un taux dérisoire, 6 Francs. « Il faut douze heures de travail quotidien pour rentabiliser un cabinet », se plaignent-elles.

12 BASIC Writing

1 Write a postcard to your penfriend.

- Ask him/her and his/her family how they are.
- Explain that you haven't written sooner because you hurt your hand and couldn't write.
- Say that you will write a longer letter soon.

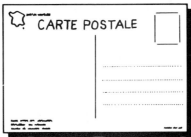

CARTE POSTALE

2 The French school participating in the exchange with your own has asked every English pupil to fill in a medical form in French. Copy the form and fill it in.

FICHE MEDICALE

Nom : —————————————

Prénom : —————————————

Adresse : —————————————

Date de naissance : —————————————

Avez-vous reçu toutes vos vaccinations? —————————————

Etes-vous allergique? —————————————

Si oui, à quoi? —————————————

Numéro à appeler en cas d'urgence : —————————————

Nom et numéro de téléphone du médecin traitant : —————————————

3 Write a letter in French of about 80 words to your penfriend, making the following points:

- You will not be at the airport on Saturday at 2 pm as agreed, because you are unwell. The doctor has ordered you to rest for at least a week.
- Ask if your visit can be postponed for two weeks.
- If it can be postponed, ask if you can be met at the same time, place and day as previously arranged, but two weeks later.

1 You have just come back from France, where you have not had the best of times. Your exchange partner, Jean-Marc, has sent you a letter. Study it carefully.

Montluçon le 8 août

Cher Patrick,

J'espère que tu vas mieux maintenant. C'est vraiment dommage. Huit jours au lit, c'est beaucoup, même pour une mauvaise grippe. J'aurais aimé que tu restes ici plus longtemps ; ce sera pour l'année prochaine, peut-être Tu comptes revenir à l'école l'an prochain ? Comment vont tes parents ? Et ton frère Robert ? J'aimerais bien le revoir. Moi, ça ne va pas très bien. Je pense que j'ai attrapé la grippe. En tous cas, ça fait deux jours que je manque l'école ! Bon, je te laisse
A la prochaine
Jean-Marc

Now write a reply to Jean-Marc's letter in French (about 100 words), making the following points:

– Thank him for his letter and tell him you are much better.

– Explain that you hope to go on the exchange again next year.

– Answer Jean-Marc's question about your family.

– Wish him a prompt recovery.

– As your parents have agreed to this, invite Jean-Marc to spend some time at your home this year.

– Say you look forward to your next meeting.

2 Study the picture below and write the story in French (about 100 words). Relate the story as if you were Paul, if you wish.

Useful vocabulary:
un brancard – a stretcher
un plâtre – a plaster
sur la touche – on the touchline

ANPE
Agence Nationale
Pour l'Emploi

EMPLOYMENT

1 Listen carefully to the tape, which is in short sections. You will hear each item twice, then answer the questions below.

Section 1

What is your French penfriend asking you?

Section 2

How will the speaker spend the money he has earned?

Section 3

How many hours a day does this job involve?

Section 4

What is the hourly rate of pay for this job?

Section 5

How long is the coffee-break?

Section 6

What first step must you take if you are ill and cannot go to work?

Section 7

What is the careers officer asking the applicant?

2 Copy this job interview form into your exercise book, then listen carefully to the interview, which is in two sections, and fill in the details. You will hear the dialogue twice.

INTERVIEW

┌─ SECTION 1 ─────

Name ....

Nationality ....

Length of stay in France ....

Address in France ....

....

Transport to work ....

┌─ SECTION 2 ─────

Experience ....

....

Last salary ....

Salary offered ....

Hours of work ....

Working days ....

Starting day of work ....

---

3 John is asking his penfriend André about casual employment in France. Listen carefully to their conversation, which you will hear twice, then answer the questions below.

1 What is the best time of year to find a casual job in France?

2 Give three examples of jobs that might be available.

3 At what time in the morning does the working day start? Why so early?

4 How many hours a day could one expect to work?

5 Last year, André worked quite near his home. How did he travel to work? How long did the journey take?

1 Copy the table below into your exercise book. Listen carefully to the tape, which is in four short sections. Each section will be heard twice. In each one, a person talks about his/her job. Fill in the details you hear.

	Nature of the job	Does the speaker: like his/her job? tolerate it? want to change it?	Advantages of the job	Disadvantages of the job
SECTION 1				
SECTION 2				
SECTION 3				
SECTION 4				

2 Listen carefully to the following conversation. These two young people are talking about their plans for the future. You will hear the conversation twice, then answer the questions below.

Section 1

1 Why does Pierre think that he needs to start work?

2 What are his reservations about leaving school?

3 What are his reservations about staying on at school?

Section 2

4 What has Jean-Luc decided to do after his exams?

5 What problem does he envisage?

6 How does he hope this problem will be solved?

7 How does he feel about further studies?

Répondez aux questions.

1 Qu'est-ce que vous voulez faire comme travail plus tard?

2 Qu'est-ce que votre père fait dans la vie? Et votre mère?
Vous avez des frères et des soeurs? Si oui, qu'est-ce qu'ils font?

3 Qui coupe les cheveux?

4 Qui travaille à l'école?

5 Qui travaille à l'hôpital?

6 Qui s'occupe de vos dents?

7 Qu'est ce qu'un boulanger fait?
un boucher fait?
un charcutier fait?
un épicier fait?
un pâtissier fait?
un pharmacien fait?
un libraire fait?

2 Work in pairs. One of you plays an English student whose French penfriend has got a grape-picking job for the summer. The penfriend has arranged with his/her employer that the English student can be offered a job too. The other plays the French employer, who wants to speak to the English student on the phone.

EMPLOYER	ENGLISH STUDENT
Votre nom et adresse?	Give your full name and address.
Vous comptez rester longtemps en France?	Say how long you are going to be in France.
Bien.	Ask how much money you will make in four weeks.
A peu près 4000 francs. Où allez-vous loger?	Say that you will stay at your penfriend's for that time. Give his address.

Now swap roles with your partner and repeat the exercise.

3 Study the table below. It indicates when summer jobs are available in France, where there are likely to be vacancies, the type of work involved, and the money you can expect to make.

Période	Région	Travail	Paye de l'heure
1/10-31/10	nord-ouest		23F 50
15/9-15/10	sud		25F
10/7-30/7	sud-est		27F 25
31/7-31/8	ouest		31F 50

Now answer the questions.

1 Pour un travail au mois d'août, dans quelle région devez-vous chercher?

2 Pour ramasser les tomates, on vous paie combien?

3 Le ramassage des pommes se fait à quel mois? Dans quelle région?

4 Combien est-on payé pour ramasser les poires?

5 Combien de temps dure la saison des poires?

6 Qu'est ce qu'on peut faire en octobre dans le sud? Quelle est la paye?

Répondez aux questions.

1 Qu'est-ce que vous ferez quand vous quitterez l'école?

2 Avez-vous l'intention de continuer vos études?

3 Si oui, où? Quelles matières allez-vous étudier? Donnez les raisons de votre choix.

4 Si non, allez-vous chercher du travail? Qu'est-ce que vous aimeriez comme travail?

5 Est-ce que vous travaillez déjà le samedi?

6 Si oui, ça consiste en quoi, votre travail? Vous êtes bien payé? Combien d'heures faites-vous?

7 Si non, est-ce que vous avez de l'argent de poche? Combien? Qui vous le donne? Comment le dépensez-vous?

8 Si vous étiez riche, travailleriez-vous? Pourquoi (pas)?

9 Si vous étiez au chômage, comment rempliriez-vous vos journées?

Study the picture below and then answer the questions.

1 Qu'est-ce que fait chacun des deux coiffeurs?

2 Quel est le métier de l'homme à qui on coupe les cheveux?

3 Qu'est-ce qu'on peut acheter dans ce salon de coiffure?

4 Combien de clients attendent leur tour?

5 Qu'est-ce qu'ils font pour faire passer le temps?

6 Dites le métier d'au moins un des clients qui attendent.

7 Que fait le caissier?

8 Quel est le métier de l'homme qui répare la prise électrique?

1 This is the title of a brochure giving information about summer jobs in France.

1 What are the four main questions it answers?

2 What kind of summer jobs are often available?

3 If you applied for a job in a hospital, you would probably not be successful. Why?

---

un emploi

pour l'été?

CE QUE VOUS DEVEZ SAVOIR

De plus en plus nombreux sont les jeunes qui aimeraient trouver un "petit boulot" pendant leurs vacances.

Mais comment s'y prendre ?
Où chercher ?
A partir de quel âge a t-on le droit de travailler ?
Combien gagne t-on ?

Emplois saisonniers dans les hôtels, restaurants, cafés

Les travaux saisonniers agricoles

LES HOPITAUX
Certains hôpitaux emploient du personnel temporaire pendant l'été. Ces emplois sont souvent accordés en priorité aux étudiants en médecine et en pharmacie.

2
1 If you wanted to become an *au pair*, which telephone number would you ring?

2 As you would not be paid, how would your services be rewarded?

3 For which jobs are young ladies only invited to apply?

4 If you applied for the barmaid position, would you be given the job?

5 If you applied for the secretarial position, you would not be given the job. Why?

6 One of the jobs advertised is part-time. How and when can an appointment be made to discuss this position?

Key
JF = *jeune fille*
JG = *jeune gens*
enft = *enfant*
T = *téléphone*
voit = *voiture*
ap. midi sem. = *après-midi par semaine*

OFFRE EMPLOI

55F

Société nouvelle bdx cherche **secretaire** commerc. exper. 30 ans minim. Ecrire au journal Carillon 33 n° 560 123 qui trans

Agence publicité rech **JF** min 18 ans bonne présent. vente par tél. formation assurées forte commission se présenter mardi, mercredi, HB 24 crs de l'intendance 1er et. droite Bdx

St ADD rech 2 chefs d'équipe H ou F connais. le démarchage à domicile fixe + % + primes. Se présenter de 9 h à 11 h, 20 rue des Augustins Bdx près Victoire

Trans diffusion rech JG, JF pour vente articles de décoration en porte à porte, vendeurs confirmés uniqu. poss. de devenir chef d'equipe. Se présenter ts les jours de 8 h à 8 h 30 au Café Le Gaulois Pl de la Victoire, demandez Herve

Cherche **jeune fille** au pair pour enft 2 ans, pendant 4 mois aux Arcs (Alpes) voyage payé, nourrie, logée. T. 56 97 26 95

Cherche **serveuses** hôtesses majeures nourrie, logée. T à partir de 14h 56 34 07 00

Imp. labo offre situat. mi temps ou temps plein à F dyn. + 25 ans, aimant contacts, poss. volt. poss. 2500F mensuel, pour 3 ap. midi sem. (fixe + % + prime essence). T le Vendredi 6 dec. de 9h à 19h Prendre RV au 56 32 04 82

The following extracts are from the brochure *Un emploi pour l'été?* The questions a teenager might ask concerning possible summer employment in France are answered in detail.

```
 quel âge peut-on travailler ?

  faut avoir 16 ans au moins pour postuler un emploi.

 pendant, le plus souvent, les employeurs exigent
 âge minimum de 18 ans.

 s adolescents âgés de plus de 14 ans ont la possibi-
 té d'effectuer des travaux légers pendant leurs va-
 nces, à condition que la période de travail ne dépas-
  pas la moitié du congé scolaire. Une autorisation de
 'Inspecteur du Travail est nécessaire.

    Moins de 18 ans :

         - durée maximale quotidienne : 8 heures
         - durée maximale hebdomadaire : 39 heures
         - le travail de nuit (entre 22 h et 5 h) est in-
         terdit
         - la durée minimum  du repos de nuit est de 12
         heures consécutives.
```

1   A fifteen-year-old would not be able to take a summer job for six weeks in France. Why not?

2   If a sixteen-year-old applied for a summer job that involved the hours 6 am–10 am and 3 pm–7 pm, Monday–Friday, he or she would not be offered the job. Why?

```
            COMMENT S'Y PRENDRE ?


  Il est préférable de commencer ses recherches très
  tôt, dès janvier.

  Il faut oser frapper à toutes les portes.
  Pensez à vos "relations" (voisins, famille,
  copains...) qui peuvent vous donner des tuyaux ou
  vous introduire là où ils travaillent.
  N'oubliez pas de consulter l'annuaire téléphonique
  (sans omettre les pages jaunes). Vous y trouverez de
  nombreuses adresses.
```

3   This section gives general advice on how to go about finding a summer job in France. Name two such pieces of advice.

```
 Procéder de façon méthodique

 . Prenez le temps de réfléchir à ce que vous voulez
 faire :

       - recherchez-vous une activité dans un domaine
       bien précis afin d'en tirer une expérience
       professionnelle ?

       - voulez-vous occuper un mois de vos vacances en
       gagnant quelques sous ?

       - vous faut-il à tout prix de quoi boucler votre
       budget ?

 . Commencez par établir la liste des entreprises et
 organismes à contacter.
```

4   You are advised to be methodical in your search for a summer job. What are you told should be your starting point?

```
 Ecrire, se présenter au bureau du personnel

 N'hésitez pas à téléphoner pour savoir si l'entreprise
 embauche pendant les vacances, à vous déplacer pour
 poser votre candidature. Adressez-vous au bureau du

 personnel et dans tous les cas, même lorsque vous vous
 rendez sur place, envoyez ensuite une lettre, de
 préférence accompagnée d'un curriculum vitae, à
 Monsieur le Chef du Personnel.
```

5   Writing, phoning, and introducing yourself to the personnel officer are ways of establishing contact with employers. Whichever you choose, what other step should you take when applying for a position?

```
 . Au pair à l'étranger
 Cette formule s'adresse principalement aux jeunes
 filles. Il faut avoir au moins 18 ans. Les séjours
 durent généralement 2 mois au minimum.

 Cela peut être une bonne façon de se perfectionner
 dans une langue étrangère sans trop dépenser
 d'argent.

 En échange d'un certain nombre de travaux (variables
 selon les familles d'accueil) vous êtes hébergé ,
 nourri, et recevez un peu d'argent de poche.

 Des formules de séjours "demi-pair" se développent.
 Vous avez moins de travail à fournir mais ne touchez
 pas d'argent de poche.
```

6   Explain the difference in working conditions between *au pair* and *demi-pair*.

ANPE

Agence Nationale
Pour l'Emploi

1 Study the advertisements below. Using them as examples, write your own advertisement to be placed in the column *Demande d'emploi.*

● B **URGENT RECHERCHE EMPLOI** magasinier auto ou aide - accepte toute offre même alimentation réponse assurée - Ecrire au journal sous le n° 32913

DEMANDE D'EMPLOI

● B **NOURRICE AYANT DÉJÀ GARDE ENFANTS** bébé cherche pour la rentrée bébé ou enfant à la journée Tél 94.43.65 avant août

● B **JEUNE FILLE 16 ANS** sérieuse, aimant beaucoup les enfants recherche un emploi pour les vacances Tél (21) 91.05.06

● B **JEUNE HOMME 21 ANS** cep horticulture cherche emploi à temps partiel ou complet Tél (21) 80.00.13

2 Write a letter in French of about 80 words to your penfriend Jean-Pierre making the following points:

– Ask if you can stay at his home for a few weeks next summer.

– Explain that you could go if you had a job there.

– Ask him if he could look for a summer job for you in his area.

– Explain that you worked in England last summer (the type of the job, how long you worked, etc . . .).

3 Your penfriend's parents have agreed for you to stay at their home over the holidays. You recently sent for an application form for a summer job in their area of France, and have just received it. Copy it into your exercise book and complete it in French.

Nom

Prénom

Date de naissance

Lieu de naissance

Nationalité

Adresse

Emplois saisonniers précédents

a) Quelle sorte de travail?

b) Où?

c) En quelle année?

d) De quelle date à quelle date?

e) Nombre d'heures de travail

f) Paye

Cet emploi

a) De quelle date à quelle date êtes-vous libre?

b) Votre adresse en France

```
-  CENTRE DE DOCUMENTATION ET D'INFORMATION
   RURALES
   92, rue du Dessous des Berges
   75013 PARIS
   TEL. : (1) 583.04.92.
   Inscriptions à partir d'août. Joindre 2 timbres pour la
   réponse.
```

1 Last year you explained to your penfriend, who lives in Bordeaux, that although you would very much like to stay with him/her, you cannot afford it. Your penfriend has sent this address, for you to write and enquire about a summer job in France. Write a letter in French of about 100 words, making the following points:

- Say that you are English and that you would like to spend the summer holidays (give exact dates) in the Bordeaux area, where your penfriend lives.

- Give your age, and say that you have your parents' permission to stay with your penfriend.

- Say that you are looking for a summer job, and that you are prepared to consider anything.

- Ask if there are forms which need to be filled in. If so, could they be forwarded to you?

- Apologise for not having two French stamps, and say you include an envelope for the reply.

- Finally, if they cannot offer you employment, ask them to suggest other addresses to which you could write.

2 Study the pictures below and relate the story in French. Your exchange partner is looking for a job.

ANPE = *Agence Nationale Pour l'Emploi*

LOST PROPERTY

1 You are answering the phone for your partner, who has had to go out. The caller is telling you that your partner's bike, which he had reported lost, has been found. Listen carefully, as you will have to pass on the news to your friend. You will hear the message twice, then answer the questions below.

1 Where is the call coming from?
2 When and where was the bike found?
3 What two things does your friend have to do before collecting his bike?
4 At what time does the office close?
5 Why is your friend asked to call in as early as possible?

2 The lost property office is on the other side of the town. You decide to phone them to find out whether your brown leather wallet that you lost yesterday has been found. It contained an underground train ticket, and 27 francs: one 20-franc note, five one-franc coins, and one 2-franc coin. Listen to what the employee says and tell him which wallet you think is yours. He will describe the wallets handed in yesterday at the office. You will hear the message twice.

3 You and the other members of your exchange party are to spend some time next week in your partner's school. The school has arranged that English pupils can benefit from the same facilities and services as the French pupils. In this morning's school *bulletin*, announcements regarding lost property were made. Listen carefully to them and answer the questions below. The tape is in sections, and you will hear each section twice.

Section 1

1 How must English pupils go about recovering lost property?
2 What role does the form tutor play in recovering property lost by English pupils?

Section 2

3 What precautions are French pupils advised to take so as to recover their lost property more easily?
4 Name three things that French pupils tend to lose easily.

Section 3

5 How often are French pupils allowed to visit the school's lost property store?
6 Where exactly does M. Chabert have lost property on display?
7 When is the end of the school term?
8 What will happen to lost property at the end of the term?

1 Work in pairs. One of you is on holiday in France and lost his/her passport the previous evening. He/she is phoning the local paper to put a notice in the small ads. The other plays the French newspaper employee.

EMPLOYEE	TOURIST
Allo, ici la Gazette Niçoise, qu'est-ce que je peux faire pour vous?	Say you lost your passport yesterday.
Bon, et vous avez déclaré ça à la police?	Say yes, you have.
Vous voulez passer une annonce, c'est ça?	Say yes. Describe the passport, giving your name and details on the passport.
Où l'avez-vous perdu exactement?	Say where you lost it.
Comment est-ce qu'on peut vous contacter?	Say where you are staying and can be contacted.
Voulez-vous autre chose dans votre annonce?	Say you want to offer a reward to whoever returns it.
Bon, alors voilà le texte. Perdu passeport britannique le 3 avril en ville. Récompense. Téléphonez à . . . C'est ce que vous vouliez?	Say yes and ask how much the ad will cost.
36 francs monsieur/madame. Vous voulez payer en argent liquide ou par chèque? Où préféreriez-vous que j'envoie la facture?	Answer the question.

2 Répondez aux questions.

1 Si vous perdiez votre portefeuille ou votre porte-monnaie, où iriez-vous déclarer la perte?

2 Décrivez votre portefeuille ou votre porte-monnaie. Dites ce qu'il y a dedans.

3 Si vous perdez des chèques de voyage, que devez-vous faire?

4 Si le commissariat n'a pas trouvé ce que vous avez perdu, où vous enverra-t-on probablement?

5 Si vous trouviez quelque chose qui ne vous appartient pas, qu'est-ce que vous en feriez?

6 Comment remerciez-vous quelqu'un qui a rapporté ce que vous avez perdu? Vous lui donneriez une récompense? De combien? Comment pourriez-vous contacter cette personne?

14 HIGHER Reading

Read this letter carefully, and answer the questions.

LE BUREAU DES OBJETS TROUVÉS
BERRE-SUR-MER CALVADOS

Monsieur,

Le premier octobre

Suite à votre visite du vingt-trois août, date à laquelle vous avez rédigé votre déclaration de perte concernant votre caméra, je suis ravi de vous faire savoir qu'elle a en effet été retrouvée.

Comme elle n'est pas en parfait état, j'ai pensé vous écrire pour vous demander si vous désirez la faire réparer en France - chose que je peux facilement arranger avec le magasin au bout de la rue et vous envoyer sa facture ensuite - ou préférez-vous que je vous la retourne dans l'état où elle est, ce qui est peut-être nécessaire pour une question d'assurances.

Si vous n'étiez pas assuré contre le vol, peut-être préféreriez-vous recevoir votre caméra dans l'état où vous l'avez perdue. Vous serez gentil de me le faire savoir. Nos frais seront éventuellement ajoutés au montant de la facture.

J'attends donc votre lettre et votre décision. Veuillez être assez aimable pour confirmer votre adresse exacte.

A l'avance, je dois vous dire que tout paiement s'effectue en francs par mandat postal.

Je vous prie d'agréer, monsieur, mes sentiments les meilleurs.

C Dupont

1. What good news is this letter giving you?
2. Apart from giving you the good news, there is another purpose to this letter. You are asked to make a choice between two alternatives. What are they?
3. Give details of the bill the lost property office might send you.
4. Give two reasons for which you are asked to reply to this letter.
5. How are you expected to settle the bill you will eventually receive?

PERDU   25F

Perdu **petite chienne beagle** avec collier métal. répondant au nom de Trompette, récompense. T. 56 63 19 25

Perdu Pessac **petit chien** genre teckel blanc et noir répondant au nom de Fripon. T 56 36 76 90

Perdu le 22.11 **chienne labrador** 4 mois, noir, Bègles. T 56 92 88 77

Perdu le 5/11 **chat** siamois verts cours du médoc gros matou répondant au nom de cow-boy. T 56 50 05 94 Récompense

Perdu à Lacanau le 15 nov. **chienne labrit** noire oreilles queue coupées tat. illisible. Récompense. T. 56 98 93 23

Perdu 23 nov. Eysines ou environ Dick fox blanc poil long taillie moy. tète tâchée de moir masque de zorro gentil. Récomp. T 56 28 25 66 ou 56 57 60 32

---

2 You are checking that the announcement your penfriend put in the newspaper is there. His dog was lost recently. The dog is mainly white, with black spots on its head. There is a reward. If someone finds it, how can your penfriend be contacted?

Your penfriend's neighbour lost her cat recently. It was a tabby. You think someone has found it. Where should you tell her to apply?

TROUVÉ   Gratuit

Trouvé **chat** tigré, 33 rue des Bahutiers Bx 4e et.

Trouvé **chat noir** quartier champ de courses, le Bouscat. Cont 56 48 58 22

Trouvé **setter** acajou male le 24/11 rue Mondésir. T. 56 02 77 20

Trouvé **jeune chien** à Bdx marron clair 50 cm de haut avec collier poil court. T. 56 93 14 78

Trouvé jeune chien noir genre **caniche** avec collier herant depuis début sept. dans Blanquefort Rés. Le Clos. T. 56 44 17 82 le matin et HR

You were visiting your partner's school yesterday, and had brought your handbag with you. Unfortunately, by lunchtime you realised that you did not have it any more. Write an announcement in French to be printed in the school daily *bulletin*. Give as many details of your handbag and its contents as you can and ask for it to be returned to your partner.

You lost your suitcase on the last day of your holiday in France. Write a letter in French of about 100 words to the lost property office. Make the following points:

- Report the loss of your suitcase.
- Say when and where you lost it.
- Describe it (size, colour, material, content).
- Ask whether it has been handed in.
- Give details of how you can be contacted.

Tell the story illustrated in the pictures below in French, in about 100 words.

ACKNOWLEDGEMENTS

Photographs

Keith Gibson p6, 43, 53, 68 (*top, bottom*), 70, 105; **Stephen Palmer** p35 (*top, bottom*), 38 (*middle, bottom right*), 39, 47, 53 (*top*), 58 (*left*), 59 (*upper middle*), 106; **Sealink** p79: (*top*); **Air France** p79 (*bottom*); **Keystone** p89 (*bottom*), 95; **Cliché RATP** p124 (*top*), 127; **Anne Andrault** p124 (*bottom*) All other photos: **Michel Gilles** Cover: **French Government Tourist Office** (*top*); **Keith Gibson** (*left, right*)

Other illustrations

Le Figaro p8 (*announcements*), 36, 37, 64 (*Toussaint*), 75, 82 (*Louez à Paris*), 83 (*Autocar pour Londres*), 91, 92 (*Football*), 93 (*A2*), 94 (*Les Résultats*); **Télé plus Cuisine** p10; **Cool** p11, 102; **Vaucluse Matin** p16, 84 (*Viviers*), 85 (*Inconscience*), 112 (*Bloc-notes*); **Inter 59** p17 (map); **Orange Bulletin Municipal 1984** p34; **Le Syndicat d'Initiative, Pau** p36 (*Le Tastecroute*), 44 (*Hotel de Gramont*), 62 (*Office Municipal*); **Office Départemental du Tourisme de la Manche** p45 (*Coutances*); **Prima** p52, 54 (*A à Z*); **British Telecom International** p54 (*Comment rester*); **French Post Office** p55 (*Philatélie Service*); **Le Magazine** p54 (*Banques*); **Le Syndicat d'Initiative, Hyères** p65; **Association des Sociétés Françaises d'Autoroutes** p63 (*En cas de panne*); **Icotecnica** p73 (*Les précautions*); **CAS** p72, 73; **SNCF** p81, 82 (*Pour les billets, Réservation*), 83 (*L'abonnement*), 85 (*période bleue*); **Rapides du Sud-Est** p85 (*En bus!*); **Le Point** p95 (*Quatre-vingt-dix jours*); **Jours de France** p95 (*La provinciale*); **Centre Départemental de Transfusion Sanguine du Val de Marne** p112 (*Important*); **Sécurité Routière** p113 (*Insolation, Mal des Transports*); **L'Express** p113 (*Dentistes,* Infirmières): **Centre Information Jeunesse Basse-Normandie** p120 (*Un emploi*), 121; **33** p121